THINH LAI'S
PUZZLE UNIVERSE

Published in 2020 by Welbeck
An imprint of Welbeck Non-Fiction Limited,
part of Welbeck Publishing Group
20 Mortimer Street
London W1T 3JW

10 9 8 7 6 5 4 3 2 1

A CIP catalogue for this book is available from the British Library.

ISBN 978-1-78739-406-3

Printed in the United Kingdom

THINH LAI'S
PUZZLE UNIVERSE

ORIGINAL PUZZLES CREATED BY THE VIETNAMESE PUZZLE MASTER

CONTENTS

FOREWORD

Of the hundreds of inventors of logic puzzles I've met over the years, perhaps the most brilliant is Thinh Van Duc Lai of Nha Trang, Vietnam.

Thinh first contacted me by email in February 2017 with a batch of puzzles for *The New York Times*. Not only were they original, the types were original – all new and wildly creative.

Over the next two years, Thinh and I developed a sort of partnership, wherein he submitted new puzzle inventions (more than 120 altogether), and I tested and helped him develop the ones I thought had the greatest potential.

Eight puzzle series for the *Times* resulted from this collaboration, including some of the types that appear in this collection.

I met Thinh only once, at the 2017 World Puzzle Championship in Bangalore, India, where he served as an official. He was thin, small, and shy. He spoke with his hand covering his mouth. It was the first time he'd ever left his country, and he'd never met another puzzle creator before. Clearly, he reveled in rubbing shoulders, for the first time, with hundreds of kindred spirits. He told me it was one of the high points of his life.

Thinh's health was always precarious. In January 2019 he went to a hospital near his home with a severe sore throat, at the age of 30, and tragically he never recovered.

I miss Thinh's emails, his ideas, and his genius. But I take some solace in knowing that he left a large trove of puzzles for fans new and old to enjoy, including the never-before-published ones you see here.

—Will Shortz

Puzzle editor, *The New York Times*

INTRODUCTION

Thinh was an extraordinary person. In his short life, he created hundreds of brand-new puzzles for puzzle-lovers all over the world to enjoy. Some of his favourite new creations, such as Candies, Bar Code, Boxing Match and Targets, appear in this book for you to share. I am so proud that he had eight sets of his puzzles published in *The New York Times*, which in my opinion is an impressive feat.

He deserves to be known as one of the leading puzzle creators in the world.

—Lai Duc Thong,
father of Lai Van Duc Thinh

HOW TO SOLVE

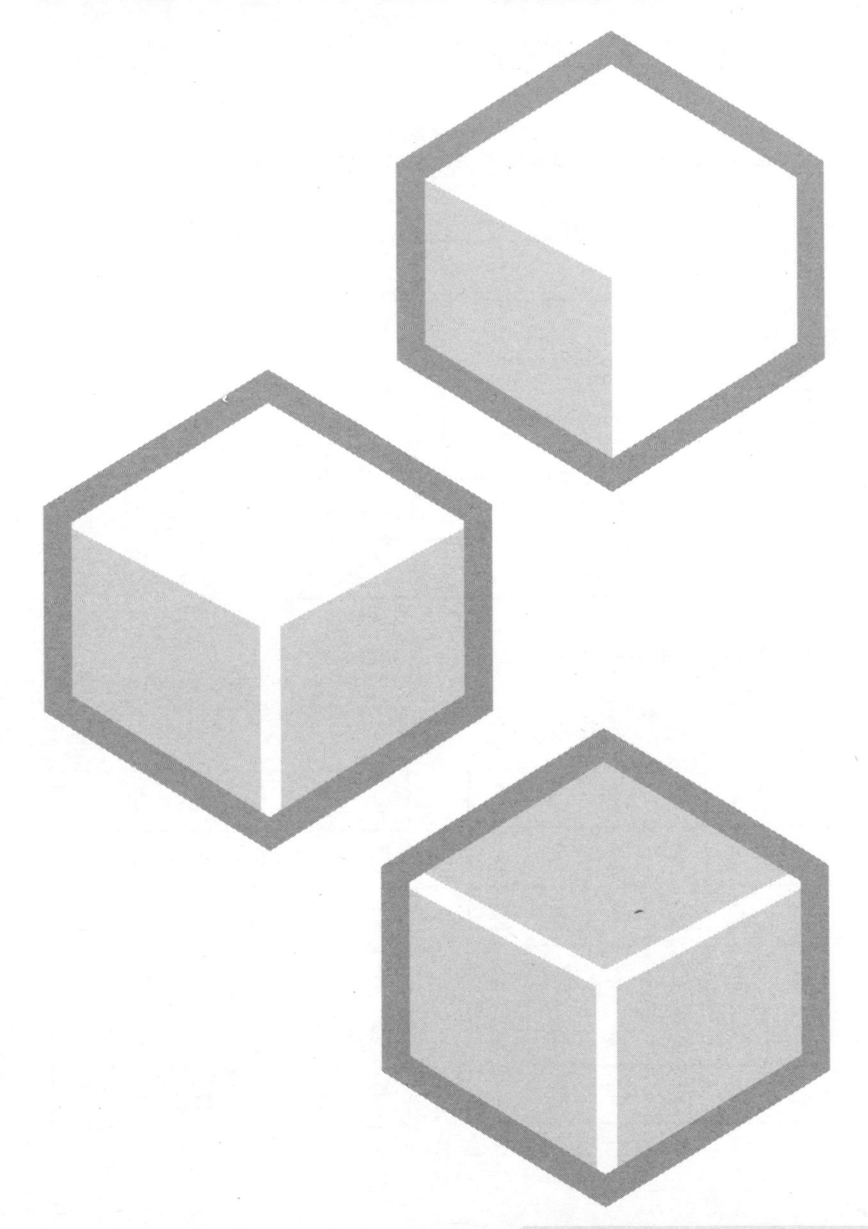

BOXING MATCH – HOW TO SOLVE

Place numbers from 1 to 9 into the grid so that the numbers in each bold-lined region are consecutive. Further, each 3x3 grid of squares in the entire puzzle grid sum to the same total.

Example

	1		2	5	
	4		4	3	
7					2
1		3	1		4
			2	4	
5		7	6	3	

Fill the blank squares with letters for ease of reference.

A	1	B	2	5	C
D	4	E	4	3	F
7	G	H	J	K	2
1	L	3	1	M	4
N	P	Q	2	4	R
5	S	7	6	3	T

Step 1

At the top left, as regions contain consecutive runs of numbers, square A must be '2'.

2	1	B	2	5	C
D	4	E	4	3	F
7	G	H	J	K	2
1	L	3	1	M	4
N	P	Q	2	4	R
5	S	7	6	3	T

Step 2

As each 3x3 square must sum to the same total, the sum of the bottom three squares of the first column (1, N, 5) must be the same as the sum of the bottom three squares of the fourth column (1, 2, 6). So, square N must contain 3.

2	1	B	2	5	C
D	4	E	4	3	F
7	G	H	J	K	2
1	L	3	1	M	4
3	P	Q	2	4	R
5	S	7	6	3	T

Step 3

Square L is part of a three-cell region containing 1 and 3 so, using the rule of consecutive numbers, square L must contain 2.

2	1	B	2	5	C
D	4	E	4	3	F
7	G	H	J	K	2
1	2	3	1	M	4
3	P	Q	2	4	R
5	S	7	6	3	T

Step 4

Using the equal sum rule, the three left squares of the top row (2, 1, B) must sum to the same amount as the three left squares of the fourth row (1, 2, 3). So, square B must contain 3.

2	1	3	2	5	C
D	4	E	4	3	F
7	G	H	J	K	2
1	2	3	1	M	4
3	P	Q	2	4	R
5	S	7	6	3	T

Step 5

As square C is part of a four-cell region containing 2, 3 and 5, square C, using the consecutive numbers rule, must contain 4.

2	1	3	2	5	4
D	4	E	4	3	F
7	G	H	J	K	2
1	2	3	1	M	4
3	P	Q	2	4	R
5	S	7	6	3	T

Step 6
Using the same sum rule, square M must be 6.

2	1	3	2	5	4
D	4	E	4	3	F
7	G	H	J	K	2
1	2	3	1	6	4
3	P	Q	2	4	R
5	S	7	6	3	T

Step 7
Using the same sum rule, 2+P+S must equal 13. So, P+S must total 11, and must therefore contain 5 and 6. As P is already in a region containing 6, P must be 5 and S must be 6.

2	1	3	2	5	4
D	4	E	4	3	F
7	G	H	J	K	2
1	2	3	1	6	4
3	5	Q	2	4	R
5	6	7	6	3	T

Step 8
With the consecutive number rule, Q must contain 3.

2	1	3	2	5	4
D	4	E	4	3	F
7	G	H	J	K	2
1	2	3	1	6	4
3	5	3	2	4	R
5	6	7	6	3	T

Step 9
The same sum rule means E must equal (5+3+2) – (4+4) = 2.

2	1	3	2	5	4
D	4	2	4	3	F
7	G	H	J	K	2
1	2	3	1	6	4
3	5	3	2	4	R
5	6	7	6	3	T

Step 10

The consecutive number rule means K must be 3.

2	1	3	2	5	4
D	4	2	4	3	F
7	G	H	J	3	2
1	2	3	1	6	4
3	5	3	2	4	R
5	6	7	6	3	T

Step 11

Using the same sum rule, 4+G+2 must equal 3+3+6. Therefore, G must contain 6.

2	1	3	2	5	4
D	4	2	4	3	F
7	6	H	J	3	2
1	2	3	1	6	4
3	5	3	2	4	R
5	6	7	6	3	T

Step 12

7+6+H must equal 5+6+7. Therefore, H must contain 5.

2	1	3	2	5	4
D	4	2	4	3	F
7	6	5	J	3	2
1	2	3	1	6	4
3	5	3	2	4	R
5	6	7	6	3	T

Step 13

Using the 3x3 square sum rule, each 3x3 square must sum to the same total as the bottom left square. So, each 3x3 square must equal 35 (1+2+3+3+5+3+5+6+7). So, J must contain (35-1-3-2-4-2-4-6-5), or 8.

2	1	3	2	5	4
D	4	2	4	3	F
7	6	5	8	3	2
1	2	3	1	6	4
3	5	3	2	4	R
5	6	7	6	3	T

Step 14
2+D+7 must equal 2+4+8. Therefore, D must be 5.

2	1	3	2	5	4
5	4	2	4	3	F
7	6	5	8	3	2
1	2	3	1	6	4
3	5	3	2	4	R
5	6	7	6	3	T

Step 15
Using the 3x3 square sum rule, F must equal 4, R equals 5 and T equals 4.

2	1	3	2	5	4
5	4	2	4	3	4
7	6	5	8	3	2
1	2	3	1	6	4
3	5	3	2	4	5
5	6	7	6	3	4

MATH BOX - HOW TO SOLVE

Place numbers from 1 to 6 into the grid so that no two numbers appear in the same row or column. Each bold-lined region contains mathematical operations – these must be calculated to solve the puzzle and the questions within – and arrows. The double arrows indicate the direction that the operations must be calculated in, and also represent an equals sign. The single arrows indicate where two digits are joined to create a two-digit number.

Example

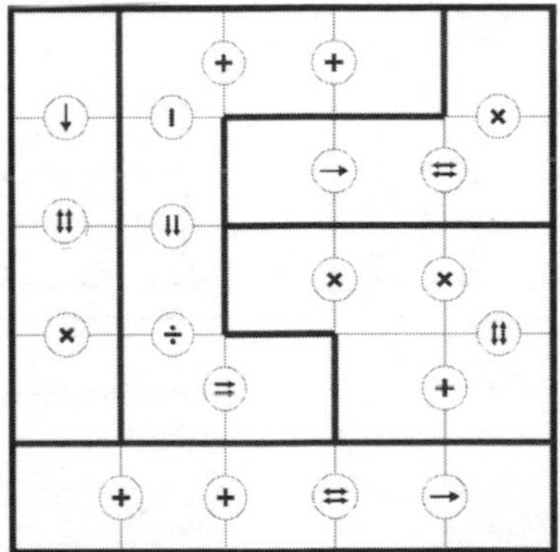

Step 1

The maximum value of the sum of three different numbers (from 1 to 5) is 3+4+5=12. In the grid, we can see that A is the tens digit of the sum of three numbers in row five, so A must be 1, and the number to the right of A must be 2 (as each number appears only once in each row or column).

For both B and C, the two-digit product of two different numbers in the same row or column must be either 3x4, 3x5 or 4x5. The product of 4x5 is 20, and as we don't use 0 in the grid, we can discard this option. Therefore, with the options reduced to 3x4 and 3x5, both B and C must be 1.

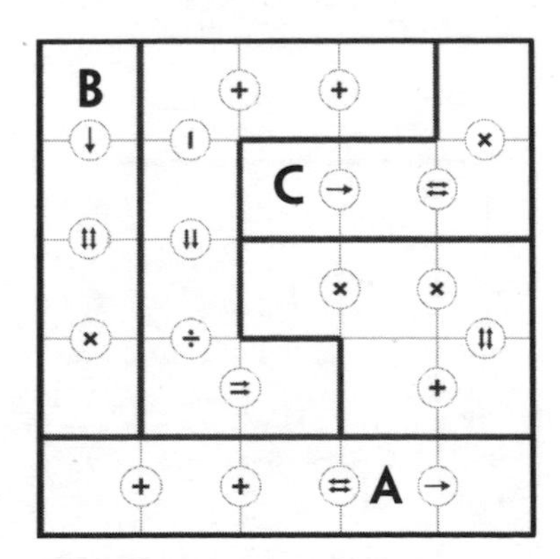

Step 2

At this point, as suggested in step 1, B and C must be 3 and 4, or 3 and 5. With the 3 and 5 option, the product will be 15, meaning two occurrences of 5 in the same row or column. So, B and C must be 3 and 4.

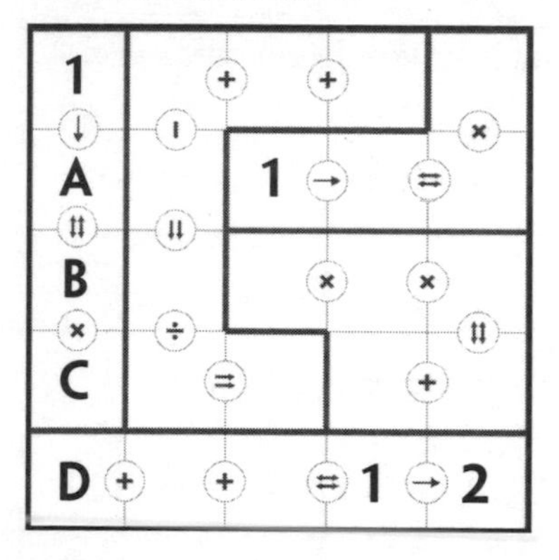

Step 3a

Here, AxB=1C, so AxB must be either 3x4 or 3x5. Looking to the left of the second row, we can see that 2 already occurs in that row, so AxB must be 3x5 (or 5x3), and C must be 5. B cannot now be 5, so B is 3, and A is therefore 5.

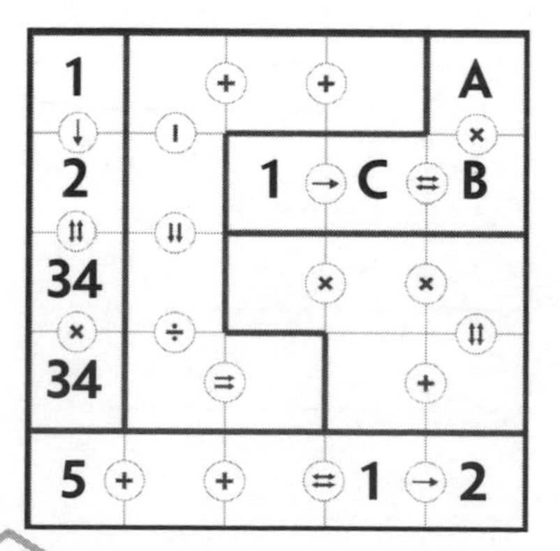

Step 3b

The second and fifth rows can now be completed.

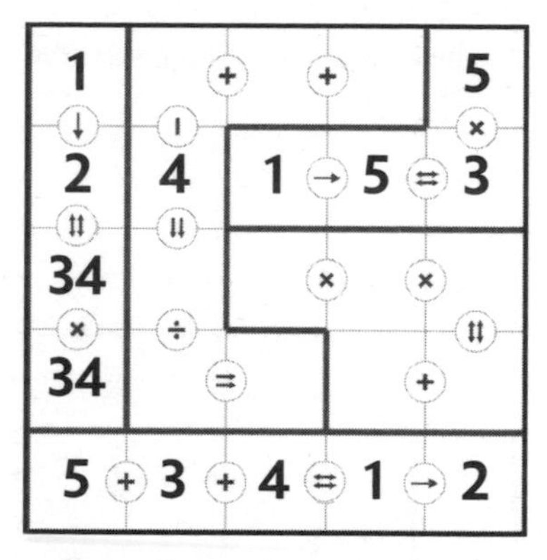

Step 4

The maximum value of the sum of two different numbers is 9 (4+5). This is a single-digit number, so A, B and C must be 1, 2 and 3 (in any order) in order to sum to a single-digit number. The digits 2 and 3 already appear in the fifth column, so C must be 1, and A and B 2 and 3 (or 3 and 2).

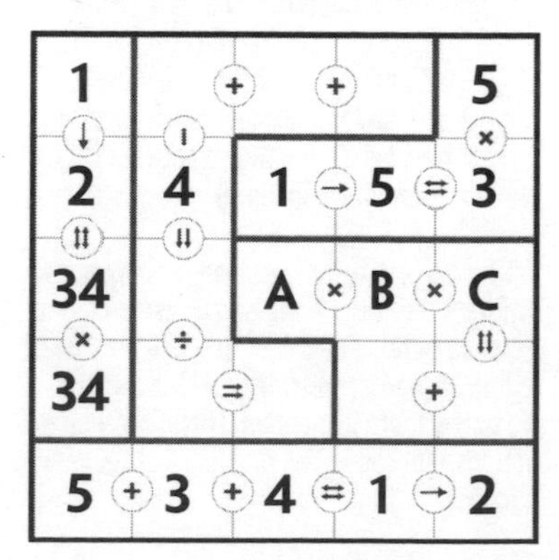

Inferring from the rules, we complete the grid:

1				5
2	4	1	5	3
4		23	23	1
3				
5	3	4	1	2

1				5
2	4	1	5	3
4	5	2	3	1
3	1	5	2	4
5	3	4	1	2

1				5
2	4	1	5	3
4	5	23	23	1
3			2	4
5	3	4	1	2

And we have the final result.

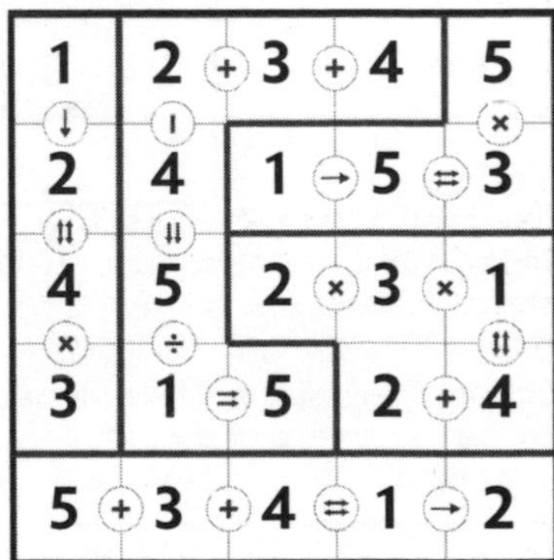

CANDIES – HOW TO SOLVE

Place numbers from 1 to 6 into the grid so that no number appears more than once in the same row or column. The numbers outside the grid equate to the sum of the numbers in their respective row or column. The numbers in each row must increase from left to right, and in each column must increase from top to bottom.

Example

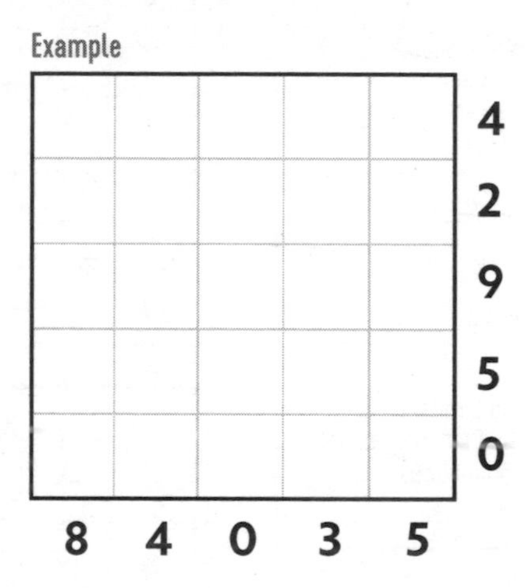

Step 1

Using the clue numbers outside the grid, we can see that there are no candies in the fifth row and third column.

M		X		G	4
N		X		H	2
A	B	X	C	D	9
E	F	X			5
X	X	X	X	X	0
8	4	0	3	5	

Step 2

Look at A and E in the first column. If A is 1, A+E must be 8. However, the maximum value of A is 5. As A+E can only be a maximum of 1+5, this is less than 8, and we can rule out this option.

Now look at the third column. If A is 2, a total of 7 needs to be produced from the remaining squares, which can only contain 3, 4 or 5 (as numbers ascend from left to right and top to bottom). This means 3 and 4 must appear in this row.

As the fourth column has a total of 3, C cannot be 4, and D must therefore be 4. Cross referencing with the fifth column, either G or H must be 1, to sum to 5. In neither of these scenarios can the first and second rows reach their totals, so A cannot be 2.

If A=3, a total of 6 needs to be produced from the digits 4 and 5 to complete the row. This is impossible, so A cannot be 3.

If A=4, only one option is available: M+N+A must be 1+3+4. However, the maximum value of N is 2 (cross referencing with the second row total), so A cannot be 4.

If A=5, the third row cannot be built, so A cannot be 5.

Consequently, A is blank.

Step 3

If B is 1, F must be 3 and E must be 2. However, if E is 2, the first column cannot be constructed, so B cannot be 1.

If B is 2, D would be 4 (as in step 2), so B cannot be 2.

If B is 3, 9-3=6 needs to be produced from 4 and 5 to complete the third row. This is not possible, so B cannot be 3.

If B is 5, the second column cannot be built, so B cannot be 5.

C+D cannot be 4+5 as the maximum value of C is 3. So, B must be a number, and must be 4.

Numerical deductions can now complete the grids 1–4.

Grid 1

		X			4
		X			2
	4	X		5	9
		X			5
X	X	X	X	X	0
8	4	0	3	5	

Grid 2

	X	X		X	4
2	X	X		X	2
X	4	X	X	5	9
	X	X		X	5
X	X	X	X	X	0
8	4	0	3	5	

Grid 3

1	X	X	3	X	4
2	X	X	X	X	2
X	4	X	X	5	9
5	X	X	X	X	5
X	X	X	X	X	0
8	4	0	3	5	

Grid 4

1			3		4
2					2
	4			5	9
5					5
					0
8	4	0	3	5	

ELBOW ROOM – HOW TO SOLVE

Draw a horizontal and vertical line from each circled number in an "L" shape. The circled number equates to the number of cells that the lines travel through in total, and the numbers outside of the grid represent the number of lines that finish in each respective row and column. The lines can never intersect.

Example

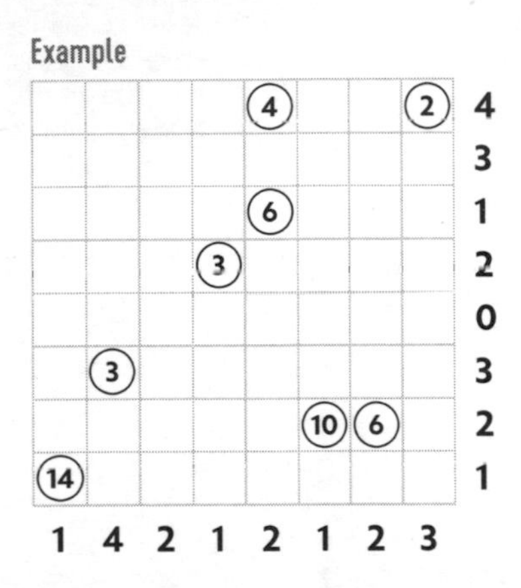

Step 1

Look at the '2' in the top right. Two lines must extend from this circle, and must total two squares. So, the lines must extend one square to the left, and one square below.

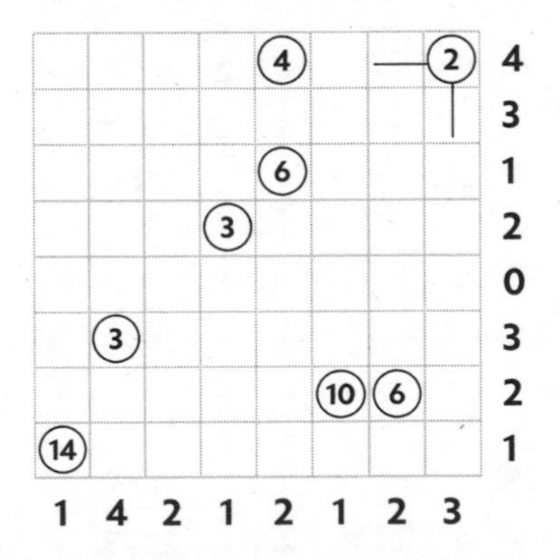

Step 2

Look at the '14' in the bottom left. Two lines must extend from this circle, and must total fourteen squares. So, the lines must go seven squares to the right, and seven squares above.

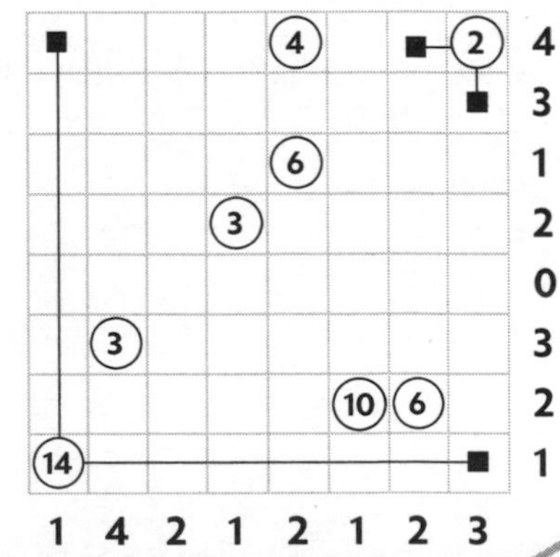

Step 3

Look at the '4' on the top row. As the lines must form an 'L' shape, one of the lines must be vertical. The only option is one square down, so mark this in. As the lines must extend across a total of four squares, the only option for the horizontal line is three squares to the left. Mark this in.

■	■			4		■	2	4
				■			■	3
				6				1
			3					2
								0
	3							3
					10	6		2
14							■	1
1	4	2	1	2	1	2	3	

Step 4

The clue number at the top of the column on the right is '4', indicating four line ends. Currently, there are three line ends (columns 1, 2 and 7). There is only one empty square remaining on the top row, so this must contain a line end. Looking down this column, this line must extend to the '10', so mark this in. This line comprises six squares, so the horizontal line extending from '10' must be four squares long. The only option available of four squares extends to the left, so mark this in.

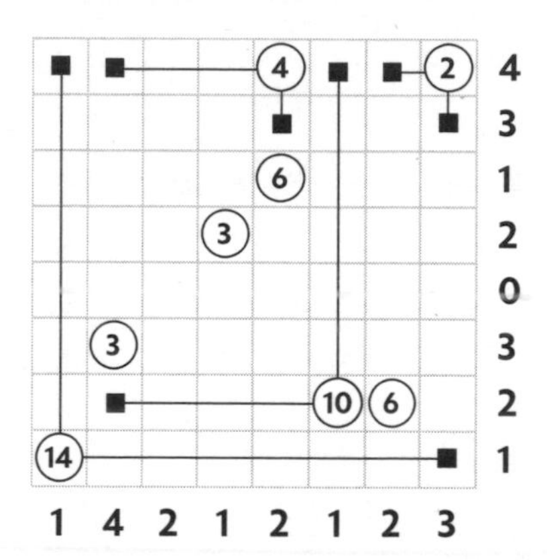

Step 5

Now, look at the '6' on the third row. There is just one option available now for two lines comprising six squares in total: three squares to the left, and three squares down.

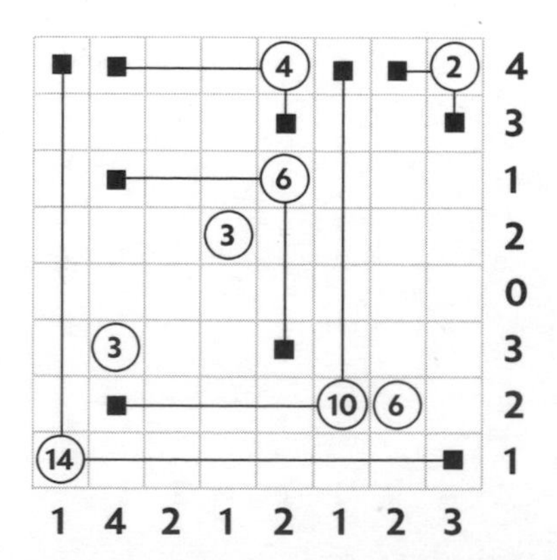

Step 6

Look at the '3' on the fourth column. There are two possibilities here: two squares to the left and one down, or two down and one to the left. If the line to the left is two squares, that makes four line ends in the second column (rows 1, 3, 4 and 7), matching the clue number below the grid. However, the '3' in the second row must have a line end in the second column, which would then result in five line ends. So, the line to the left of the '3' on the fourth row must be of just one square, and the line down of two squares. The '3' in the second column has just one possibility now, of one square to the right and two above.

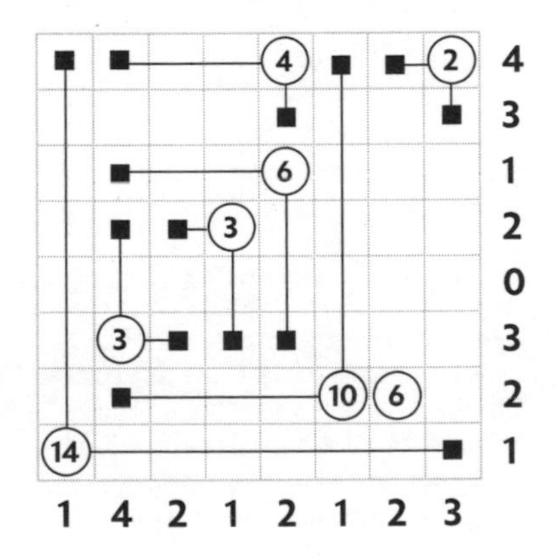

Step 7

The final numbered circle, '6' in the seventh column has just one possibility now – one square to the right and five above.

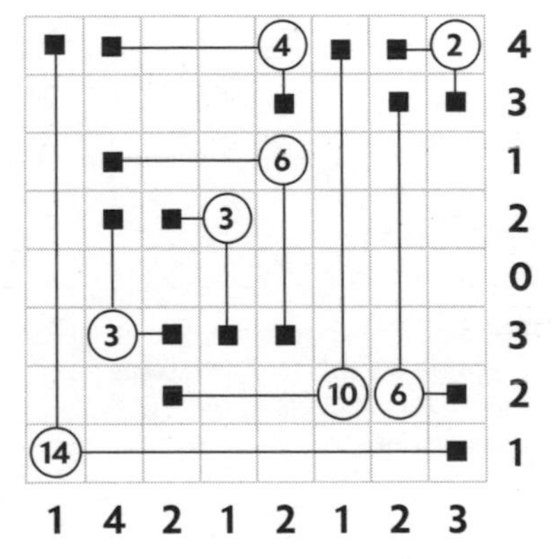

BAR CODE – HOW TO SOLVE

Add horizontal and vertical bars – no longer than the length of a single cell – to the grid in such a way that no two bars touch. The numbers outside of the grid equate to the number of bars that appear consecutively in their respective row and column. Where two or more numbers are given, at least one row or column must separate the groups of bars.

Example

	1 4	0	2	1	2	1
2,1						
2						
5						
0						
3						
0						

Step 1
The fourth and sixth rows, and second column, contain 0 bars, so cross out these options on the grid.

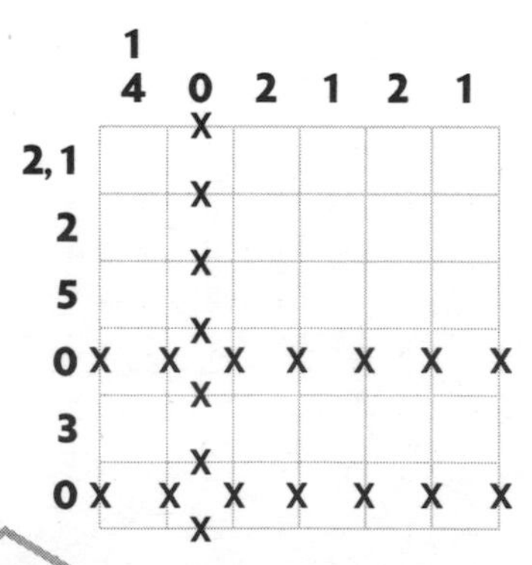

Step 2
In the first column, a total of five bars occurs (1,4), with a space between. This must mean that either bars 3, 4, 5 and 6 or bars 4, 5, 6 and 7 make up the four consecutive bars. So, 4, 5 and 6 must be bars. Mark these in.

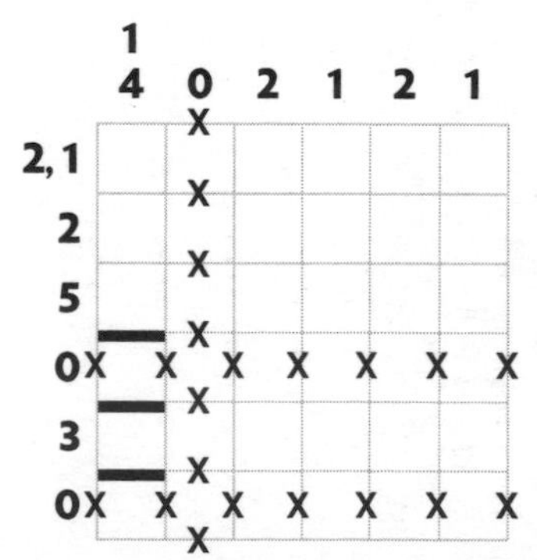

Step 3
As no bars can touch, strike through the first and second options of rows 3 and 5.

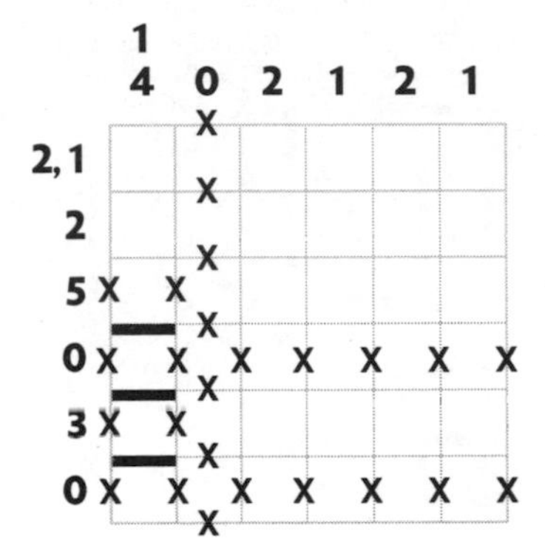

Step 4
The third row comprises five consecutive bars, and there are now only five options on this row. These must all contain a bar. Mark these in.

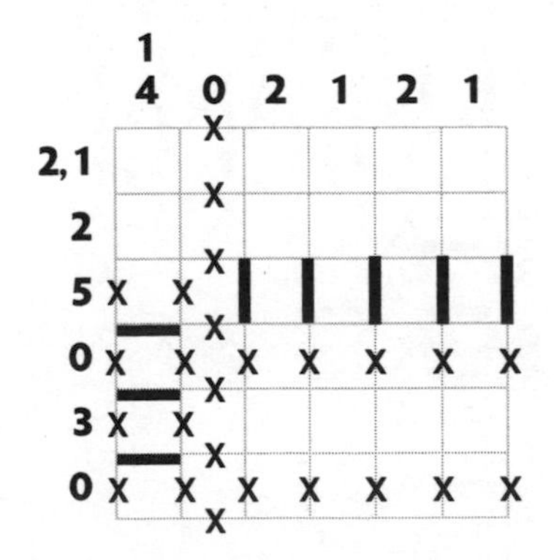

Step 5
As with step 3, as no bars can touch, strike through all adjacent options of the five-bar stretch.

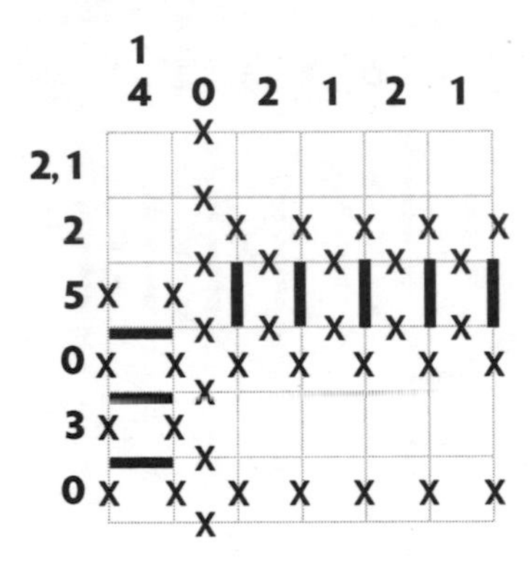

Step 6
Row 2 contains two consecutive bars, and there are now only two options left – mark these in.

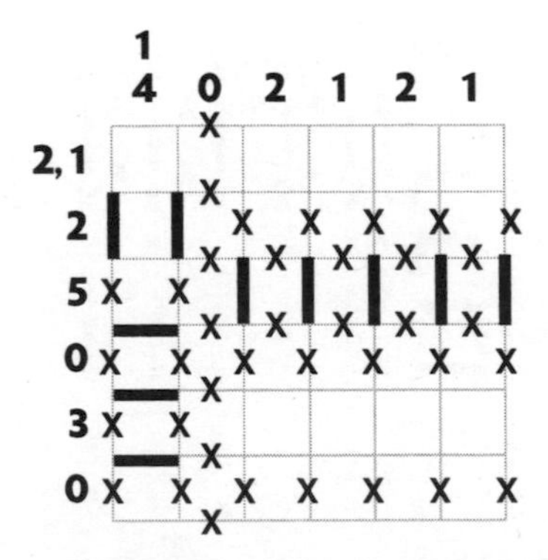

Step 7
You can now discount adjacent options to these – options 2 and 3 in the first column, and options 1 and 2 in the first row.

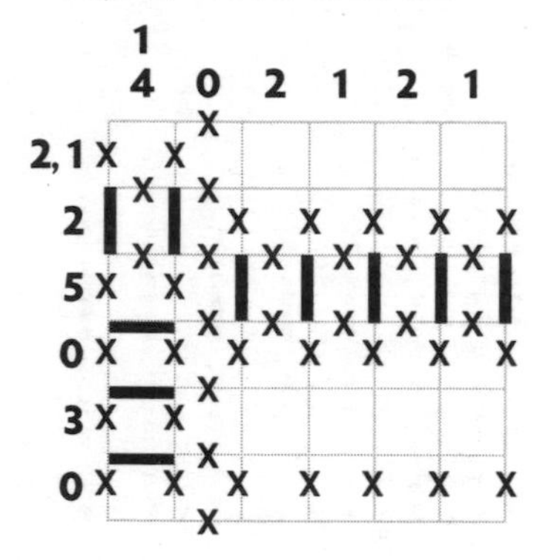

Step 8
Looking at the clue below the first column, the single bar must occur at the top of the column, and the four-bar run must finish at the bottom of the column. Mark these in.

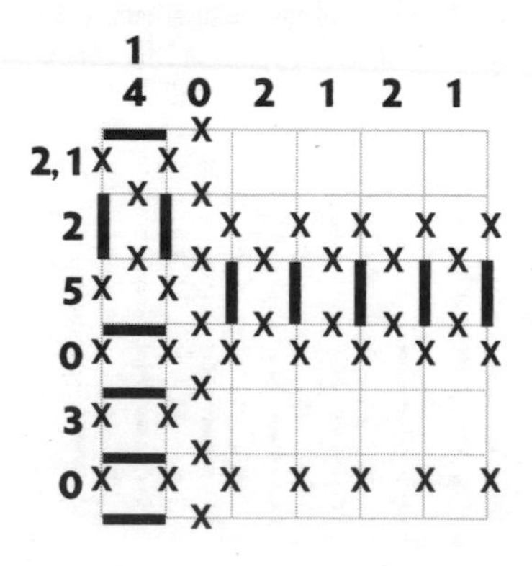

Step 9
The top row contains three bars in total (2,1). The option between the third and fourth columns must therefore contain a bar.

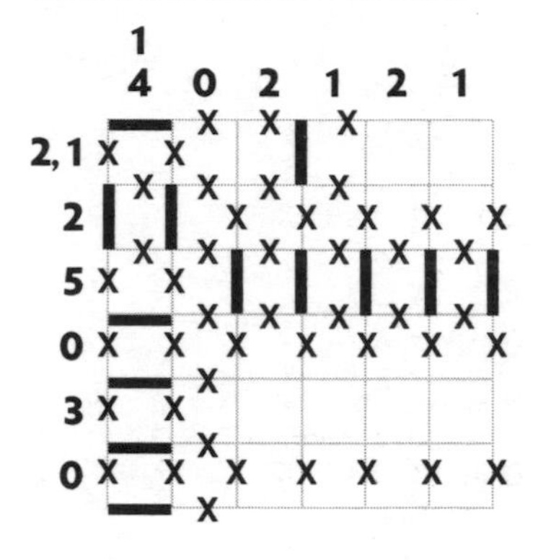

Step 10
The third column contains two consecutive bars. There are just three options left for the two bars, so the middle one must contain a bar. Mark this in, and discard the adjacent options.

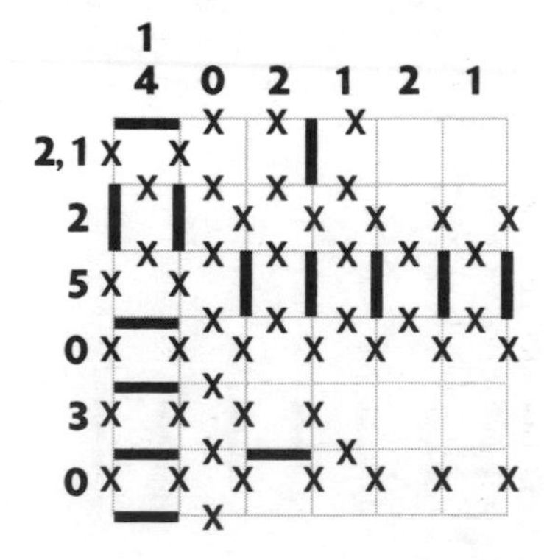

Step 11

The fifth row contains three bars, and there are just three options now available. Mark these in and discard the adjacent options.

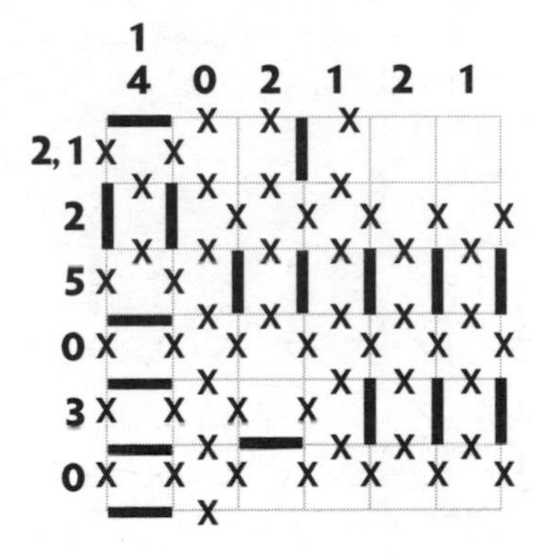

Step 12

The fourth column contains one bar, and there is just one option available. Mark this in, and discard the adjacent options.

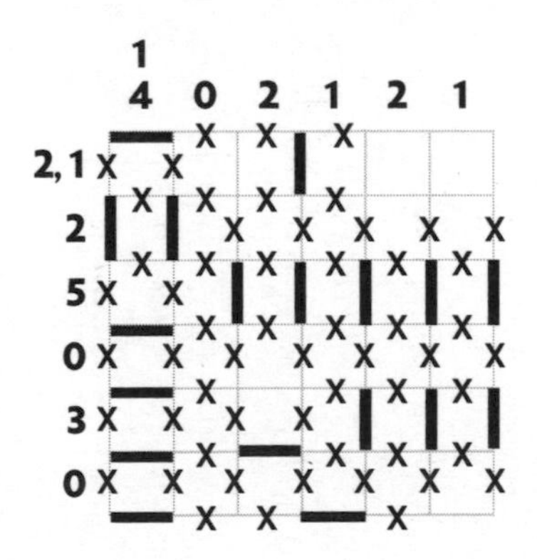

Step 13

The third column has just one available option left, so mark this in.

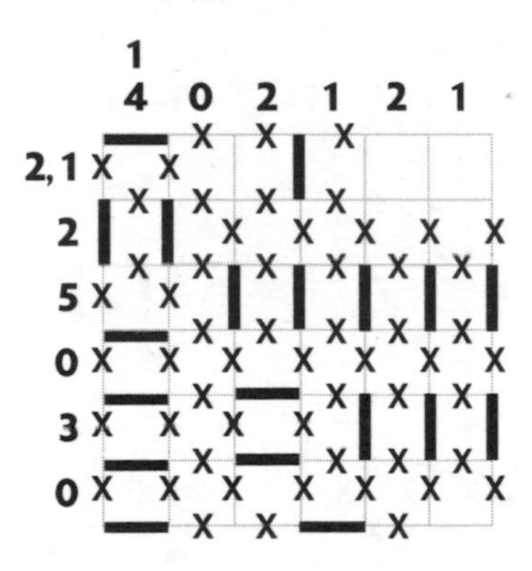

Step 14

The fifth column has just two spaces available for two bars. Mark these in and discard adjacent options.

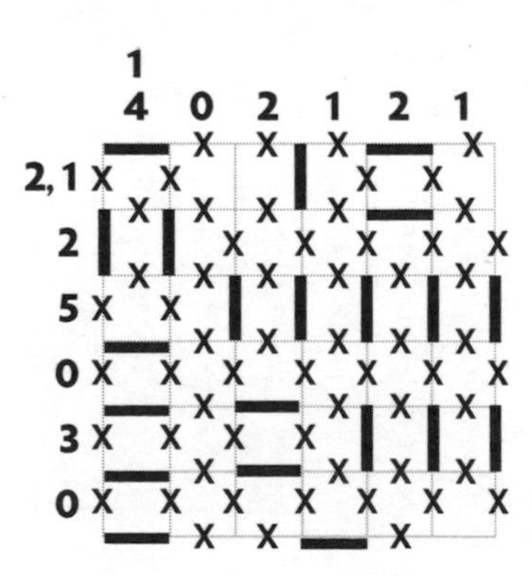

Step 15

The top row has two bars left to fill in, and just two options. Fill these in. The sixth column has just one bar left to fill in, and just one option. Fill this in.

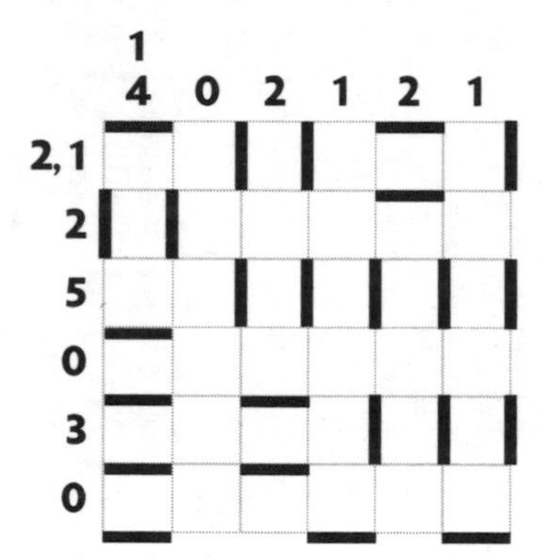

TARGETS – HOW TO SOLVE

Place arrows into the cells in the grid to complete the Targets puzzle. The numbers outside of the grid equate to numbers of arrows located in their respective row and column. The arrows can point up, down, left, right or in any diagonal and must be placed so that every target has an arrow heading towards the bullseye. No arrow can shoot through another arrow.

Step 1

The fourth and fifth columns contain no arrows, so you can rule these out. The fourth row contains three arrows, so the first three squares must contain arrows – mark these squares. At the moment, though, we don't know which direction they point in.

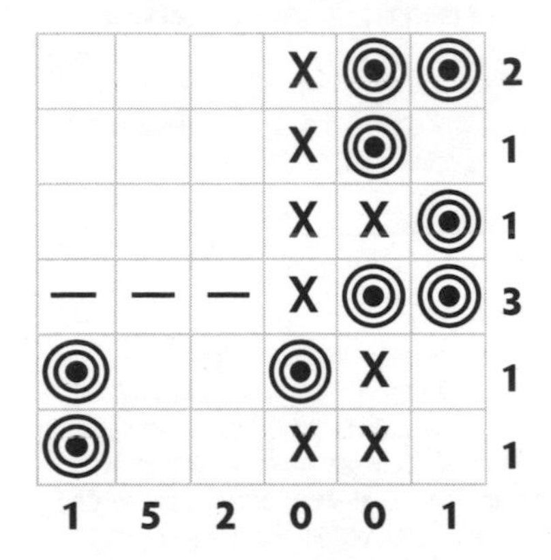

Step 2

The first column contains one arrow. From step 1, we know which square that is, so rule out the other squares in the column. Moving to the first row, this row contains two arrows, and there are only two squares left; both of these must contain an arrow – mark these in.

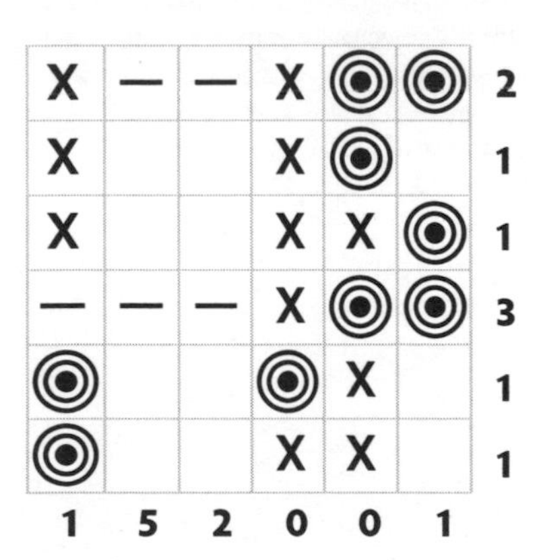

Step 3

As arrows can't shoot through other arrows, the first arrow can't point to the right. The first arrow can't point down as there is no target beneath it. The only target it can aim at is the target in the fourth row and fifth column, so mark the arrow fully. As arrows can't shoot through arrows, the square on the second row, third column can't contain an arrow. Mark this in.

Similarly, the arrow in the first column can't point right. The only target remaining is the one immediately below, so mark this in.

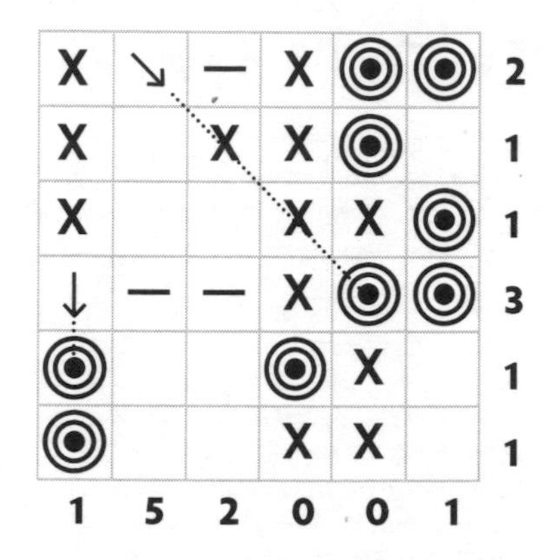

Step 4

Look at the target at the top right. There is just one route to reach this target, the second row, sixth column. This square must contain an arrow, and it must point up. Mark this in. There is only one arrow in the second row, so we can rule out the remaining square. This square is in a column with five arrows. Consequently, every other square in the second column must contain an arrow. Mark these in. At this stage, all arrows have been located, and all remaining blank squares can be ruled out.

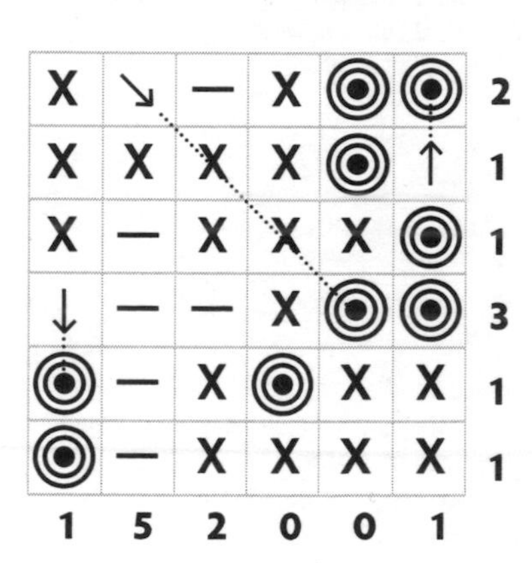

Step 5

There is just one route to the target on the third row, so we know the arrow on the third row must point right. Similarly, the remaining target on the fourth row must be aimed at by the remaining arrow on the top row. Mark these in. Repeat the process with the remaining targets: the arrow on the bottom row has just one target to aim at, also on the bottom row; the remaining target on the top row only has one arrow to aim at it, on the fourth row, second column; the target on the second row must be aimed at by the remaining arrow on the fourth row; the arrow on the fifth row must aim to the right.

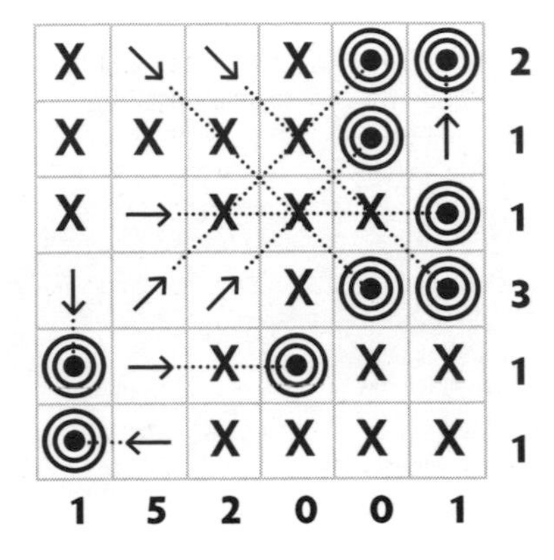

PUZZLES

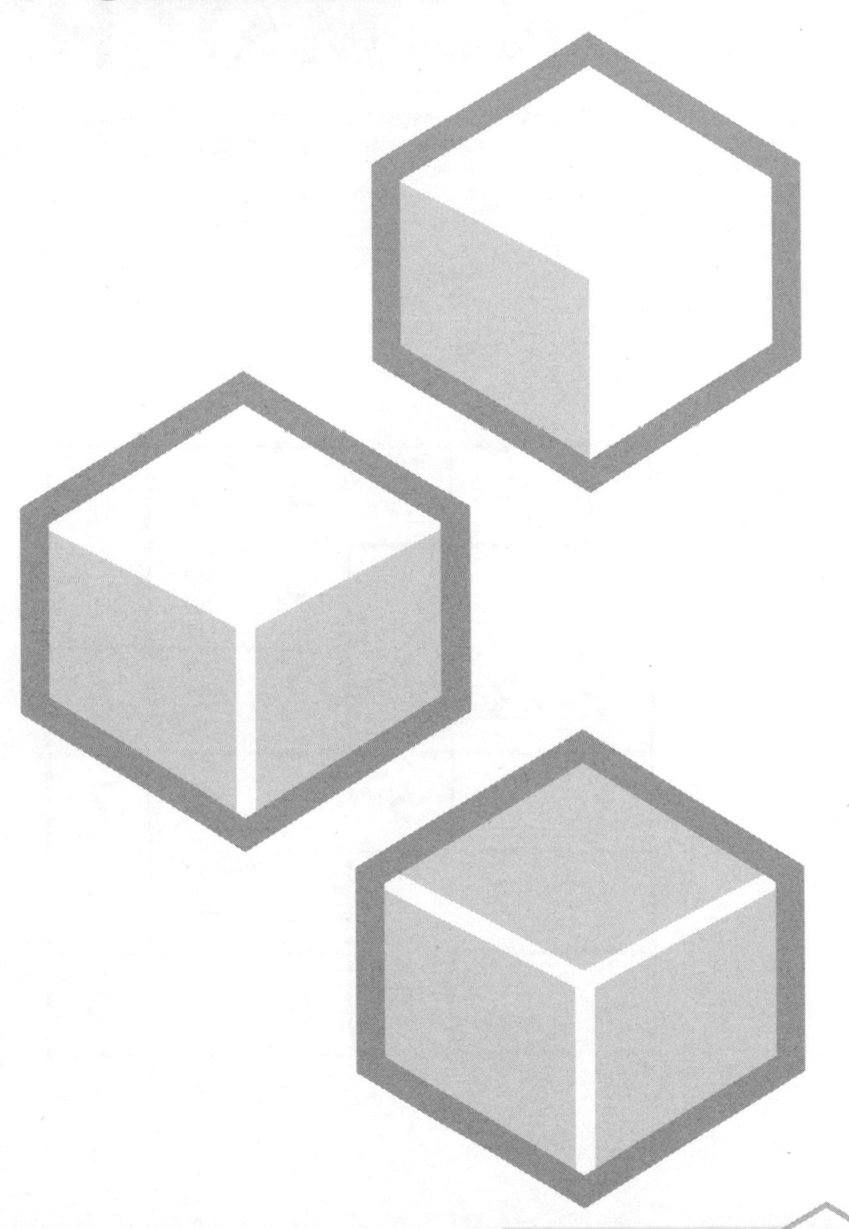

BOXING MATCH

Place numbers from 1 to 9 into the grid so that the numbers in each bold-lined region are consecutive, and so that every 3x3 grid of squares in the entire puzzle grid sum to the same total.

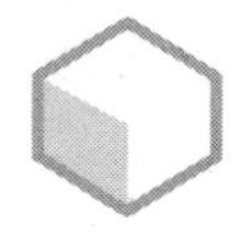

EASY

		3	4	1	
7					
	3				6
1		5		1	7
	7			4	
4		8	5		6

SOLUTION PAGE 144

MEDIUM

3		8		6	
5		3		3	4
	2		5		6
		8		8	
	6		7		3
3		5		6	

SOLUTION PAGE 144

HARD

3	5				3
		8		7	
7			3		
2				5	
	6		9		2
	7	3		8	

SOLUTION PAGE 144

CANDIES

Place numbers from 1 to 6 into the grid so that no number appears more than once in the same row or column. The numbers outside the grid equate to the sum of the numbers in their respective row or column. The numbers in each row must increase from left to right, and in each column must increase from top to bottom.

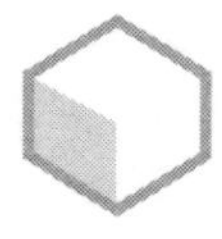

EASY

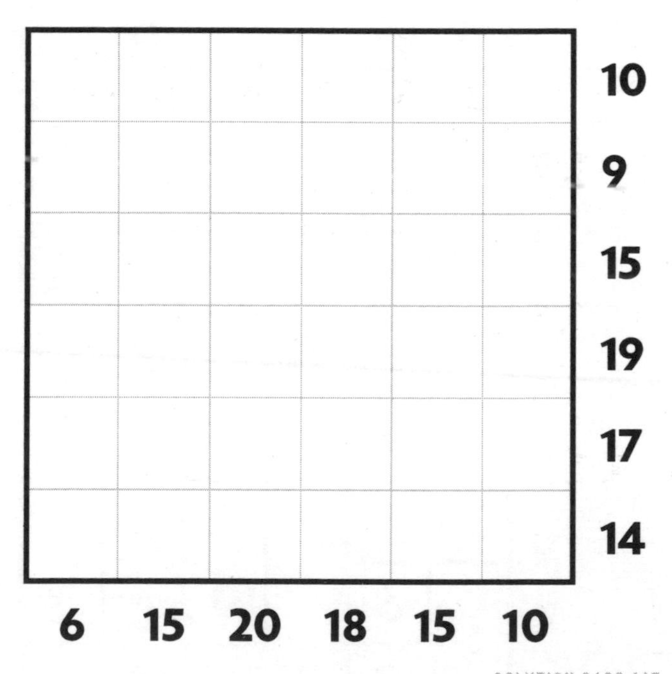

SOLUTION PAGE 145

BAR CODE

Add horizontal and vertical bars – no longer than the length of a single cell – to the grid in such a way that no two bars touch. The numbers outside of the grid equate to the number of bars that appear consecutively in their respective row and column. Where two or more numbers are given, at least one row or column must separate the groups of bars.

MEDIUM

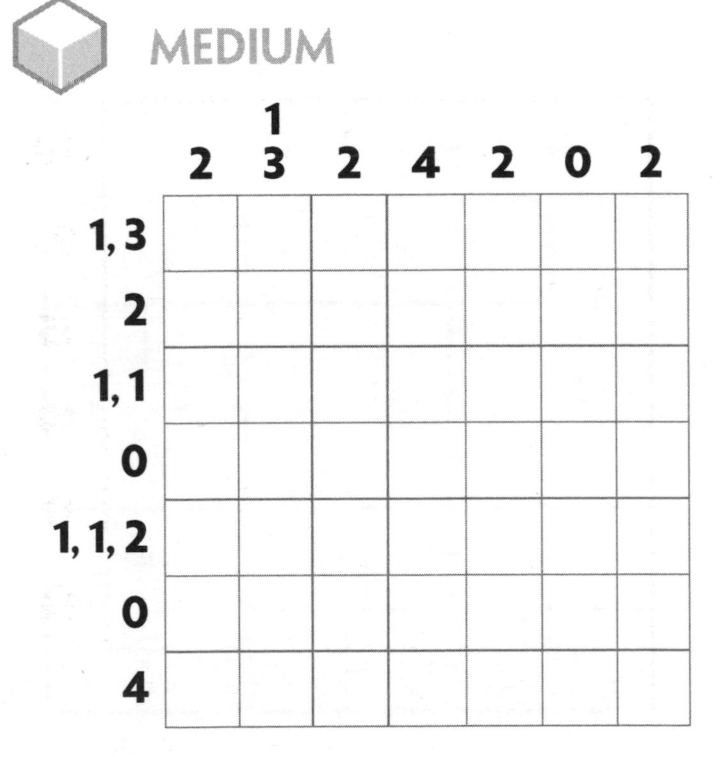

SOLUTION PAGE 145

MATH BOX

Place numbers from 1 to 6 (or 7 in the case of the Hard puzzle) into the grid so that no two numbers appear in the same row or column. Each bold-lined region contains mathematical operations – these must be calculated to solve the puzzle and the questions within – and arrows. The double arrows indicate the direction that the operations must be calculated in, and also represent an equals sign. The single arrows indicate where two digits are joined to create a two-digit number. You may also need to use brackets to complete some of the calculations.

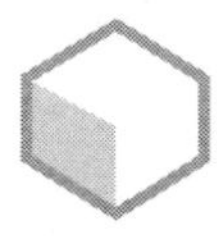

EASY

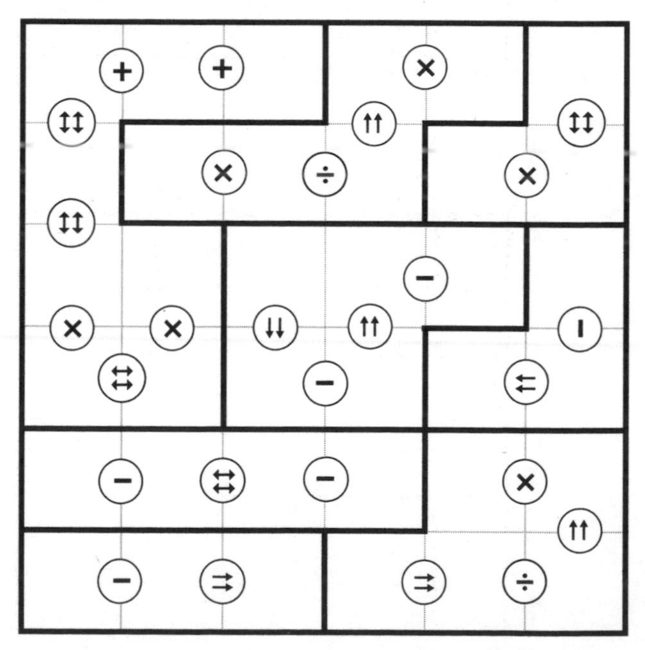

SOLUTION PAGE 145

MEDIUM

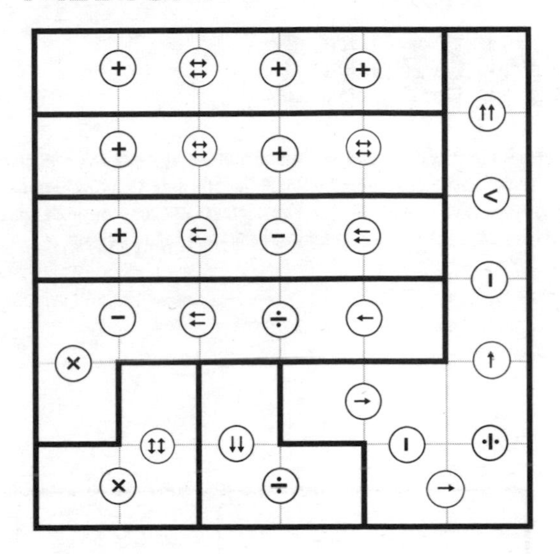

SOLUTION PAGE 146

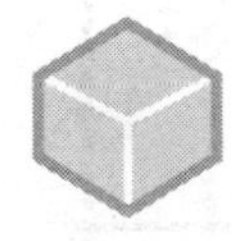

HARD

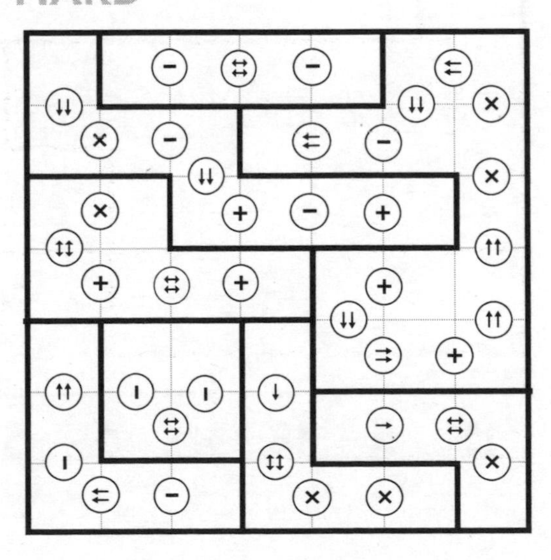

SOLUTION PAGE 146

CANDIES

Place numbers from 1 to 6 into the grid so that no number appears more than once in the same row or column. The numbers outside the grid equate to the sum of the numbers in their respective row or column. The numbers in each row must increase from left to right, and in each column must increase from top to bottom.

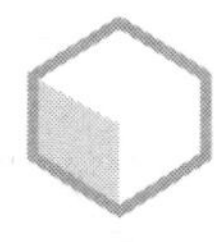

EASY

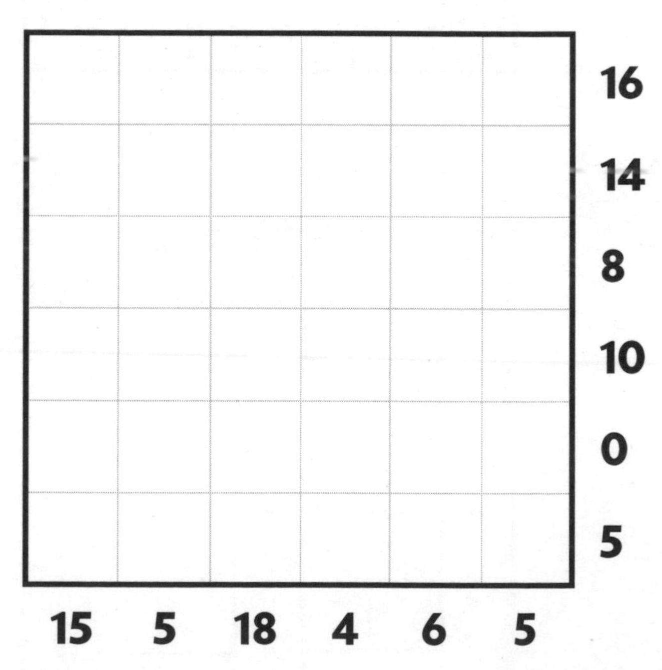

SOLUTION PAGE 146

MEDIUM

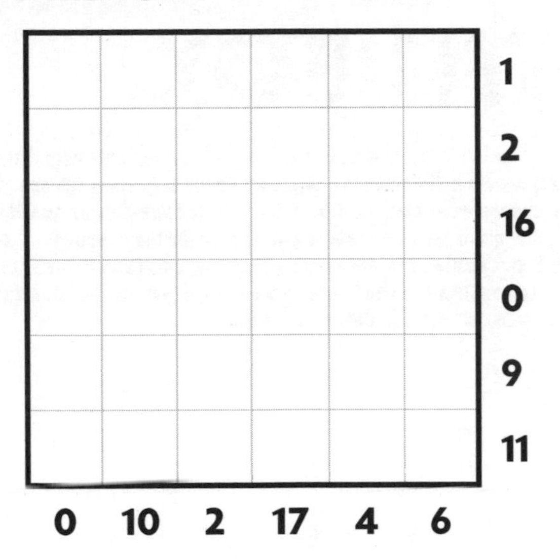

SOLUTION PAGE 147

HARD

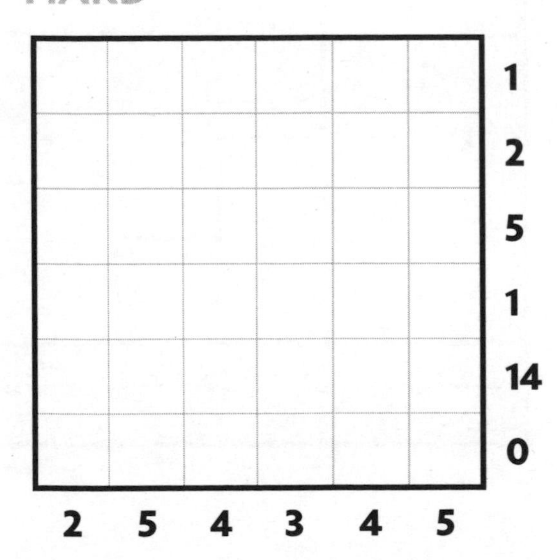

SOLUTION PAGE 147

MATH BOX

Place numbers from 1 to 6 (or 7 in the case of the Hard puzzle) into the grid so that no two numbers appear in the same row or column. Each bold-lined region contains mathematical operations – these must be calculated to solve the puzzle and the questions within – and arrows. The double arrows indicate the direction that the operations must be calculated in, and also represent an equals sign. The single arrows indicate where two digits are joined to create a two-digit number. You may also need to use brackets to complete some of the calculations.

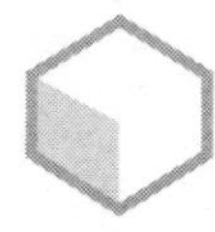

EASY

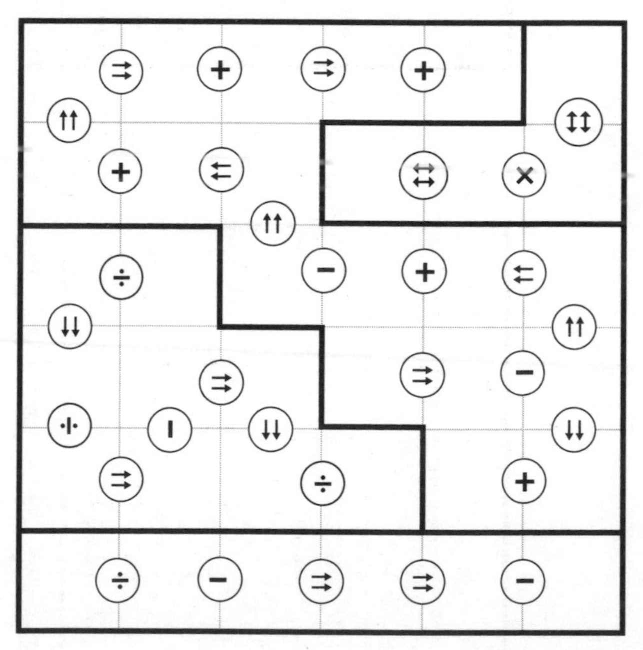

SOLUTION PAGE 147

MEDIUM

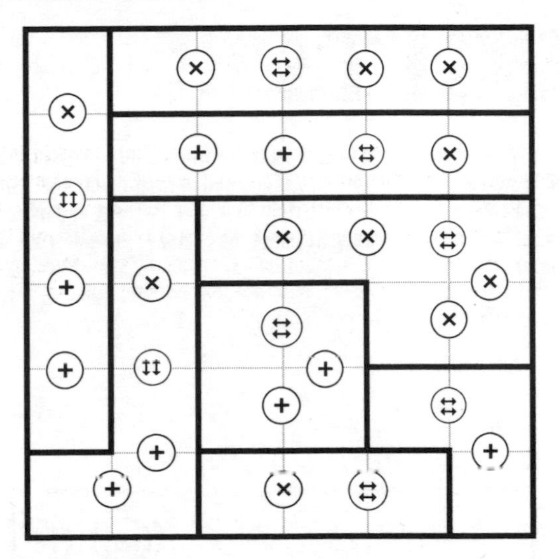

SOLUTION PAGE 148

HARD

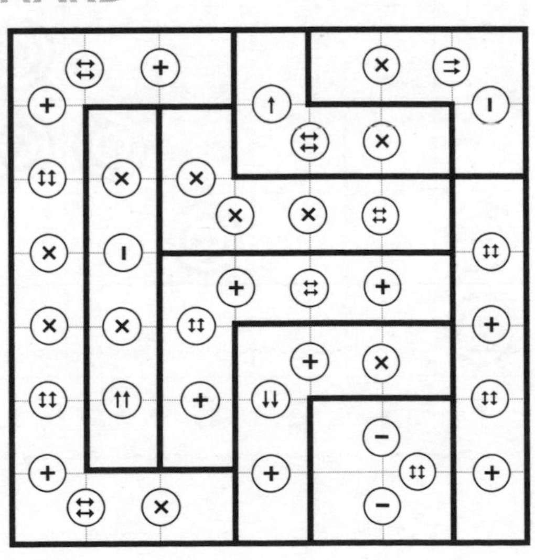

SOLUTION PAGE 148

TARGETS

Place arrows into the cells in the grid to complete the Targets puzzle. The numbers outside of the grid equate to numbers of arrows located in their respective row and column. The arrows can point up, down, left, right or in any diagonal and must be placed so that every target has an arrow heading towards the bullseye. No arrow can shoot through another arrow.

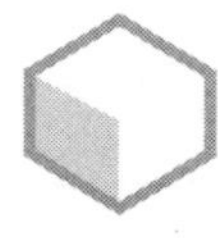

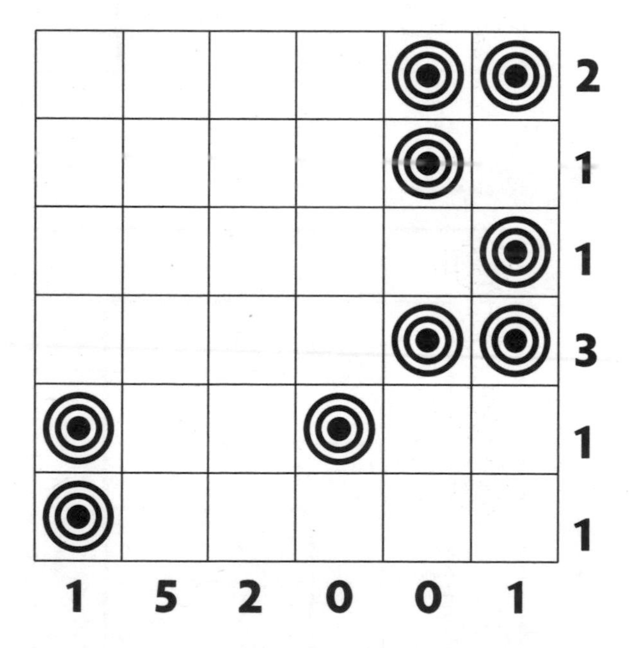

SOLUTION PAGE 148

MEDIUM

						3
	◎	◎	◎			2
						3
◎					◎	1
	◎	◎	◎		◎	0
	◎	◎				2
4	2	2	1	0	2	

SOLUTION PAGE 149

HARD

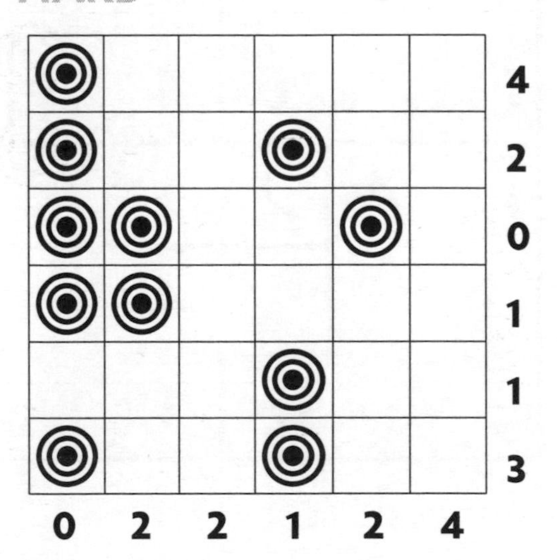

SOLUTION PAGE 149

BOXING MATCH

Place numbers from 1 to 7 into the grid so that the numbers in each bold-lined region are consecutive, and so that every 3x3 grid of squares in the entire puzzle grid sum to the same total.

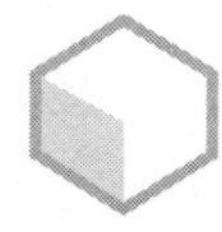

EASY

3	5		1		5
	3			4	
		6	4		6
	4	2			3
1			4	6	
		7	1		7

SOLUTION PAGE 149

BAR CODE

Add horizontal and vertical bars – no longer than the length of a single cell – to the grid in such a way that no two bars touch. The numbers outside of the grid equate to the number of bars that appear consecutively in their respective row and column. Where two or more numbers are given, at least one row or column must separate the groups of bars.

MEDIUM

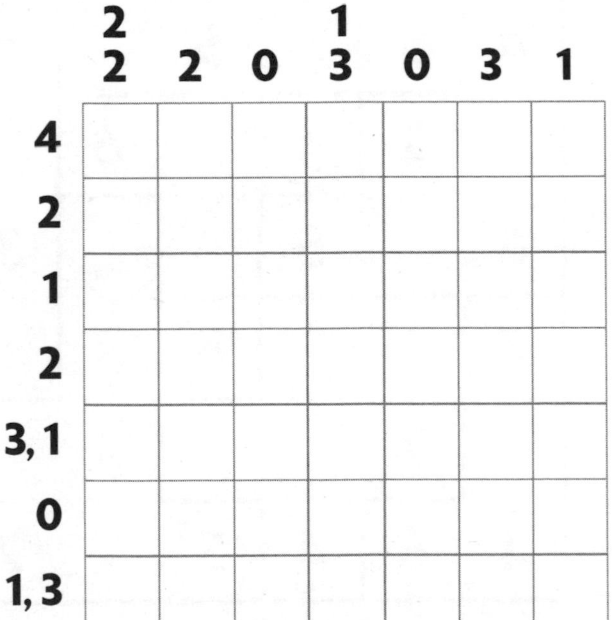

SOLUTION PAGE 150

BOXING MATCH

Place numbers from 1 to 9 into the grid so that the numbers in each bold-lined region are consecutive, and so that every 3x3 grid of squares in the entire puzzle grid sum to the same total.

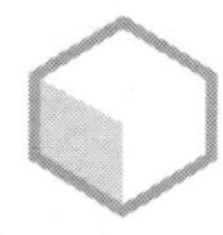

EASY

4			5		4
	2	4		6	
6		5			3
7			8	3	
	2				
4	6	4	5		2

SOLUTION PAGE 150

MEDIUM

	2		2	3	
5					2
	4	7		4	
3			4		4
	5				4
6	3		6	3	

SOLUTION PAGE 150

HARD

	2	5	6		7
8				5	
9		5		3	1
1					
	7		7	8	
		6		3	

SOLUTION PAGE 151

ELBOW ROOM

Draw a horizontal and vertical line from each circled number in an "L" shape. The circled number equates to the number of cells that the lines travel through in total, and the numbers outside of the grid represent the number of lines that finish in each respective row and column. The lines can never intersect.

EASY

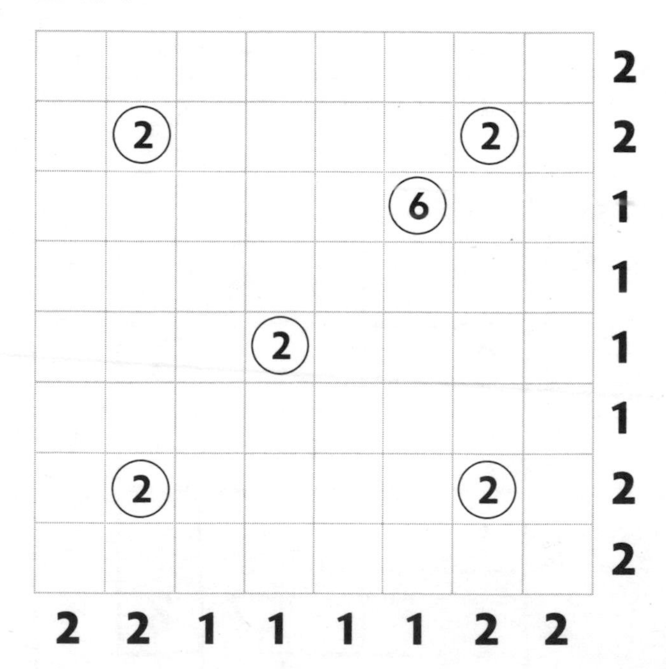

SOLUTION PAGE 151

BAR CODE

Add horizontal and vertical bars – no longer than the length of a single cell – to the grid in such a way that no two bars touch. The numbers outside of the grid equate to the number of bars that appear consecutively in their respective row and column. Where two or more numbers are given, at least one row or column must separate the groups of bars.

MEDIUM

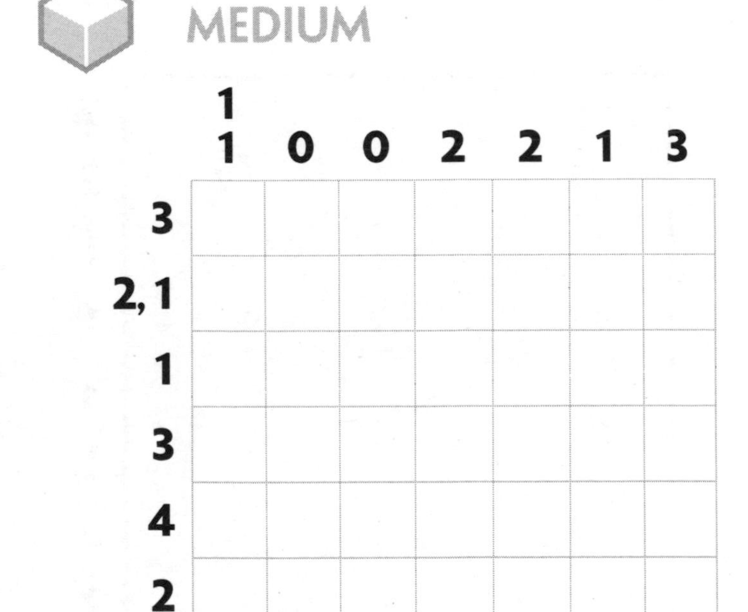

SOLUTION PAGE 151

CANDIES

Place numbers from 1 to 6 into the grid so that no number appears more than once in the same row or column. The numbers outside the grid equate to the sum of the numbers in their respective row or column. The numbers in each row must increase from left to right, and in each column must increase from top to bottom.

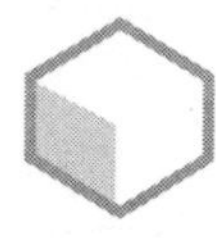

EASY

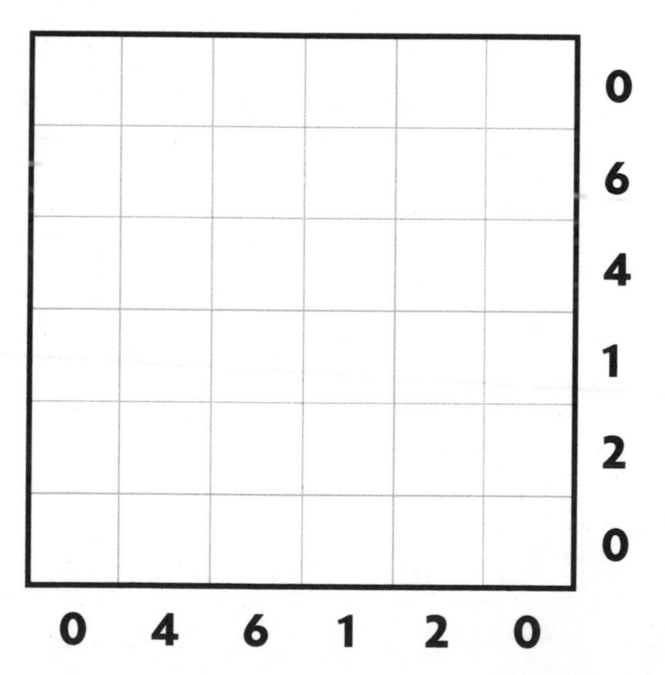

SOLUTION PAGE 152

MATH BOX

Place numbers from 1 to 6 into the grid so that no two numbers appear in the same row or column. Each bold-lined region contains mathematical operations – these must be calculated to solve the puzzle and the questions within – and arrows. The double arrows indicate the direction that the operations must be calculated in, and also represent an equals sign. The single arrows indicate where two digits are joined to create a two-digit number. You may also need to use brackets to complete some of the calculations.

EASY

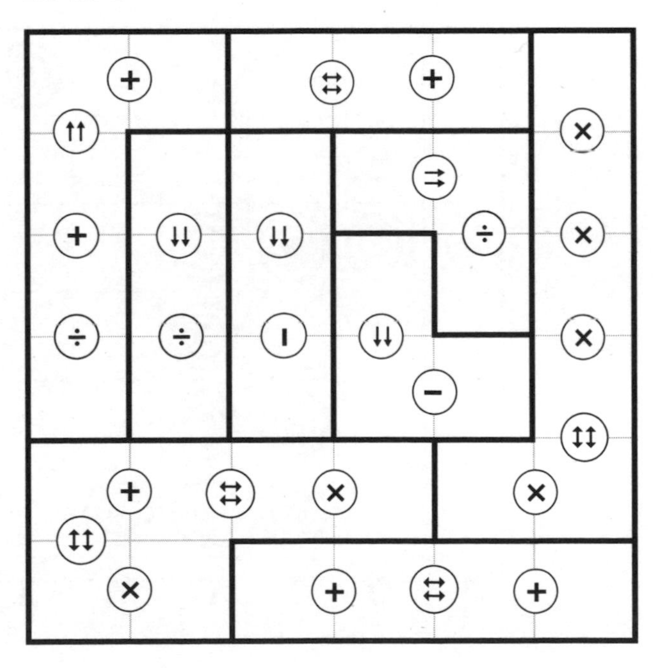

SOLUTION PAGE 152

TARGETS

Place arrows into the cells in the grid to complete the Targets puzzle. The numbers outside of the grid equate to numbers of arrows located in their respective row and column. The arrows can point up, down, left, right or in any diagonal and must be placed so that every target has an arrow heading towards the bullseye. No arrow can shoot through another arrow.

MEDIUM

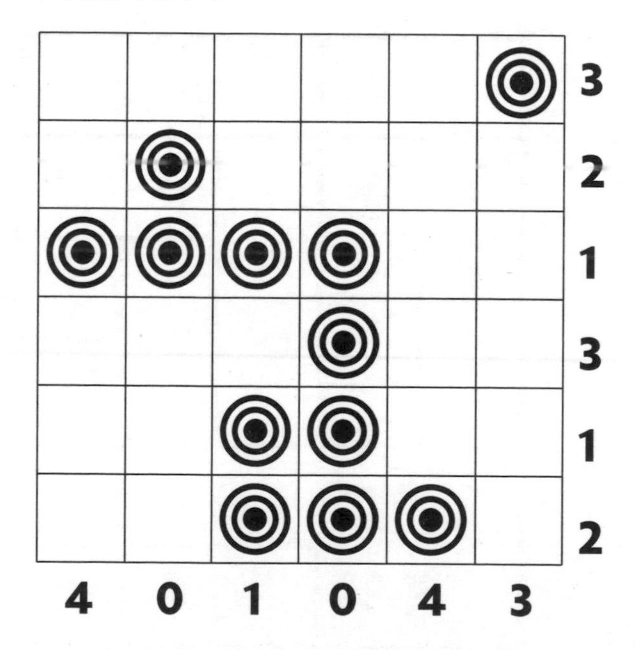

SOLUTION PAGE 152

BOXING MATCH

Place numbers from 1 to 8 into the grid so that the numbers in each bold-lined region are consecutive, and so that every 3x3 grid of squares in the entire puzzle grid sum to the same total.

MEDIUM

	4	4			
	6		3		7
5			4	7	
		6			4
3					
	8		6		3

SOLUTION PAGE 153

ELBOW ROOM

Draw a horizontal and vertical line from each circled number in an "L" shape. The circled number equates to the number of cells that the lines travel through in total, and the numbers outside of the grid represent the number of lines that finish in each respective row and column. The lines can never intersect.

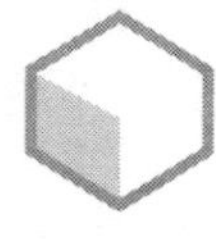

EASY

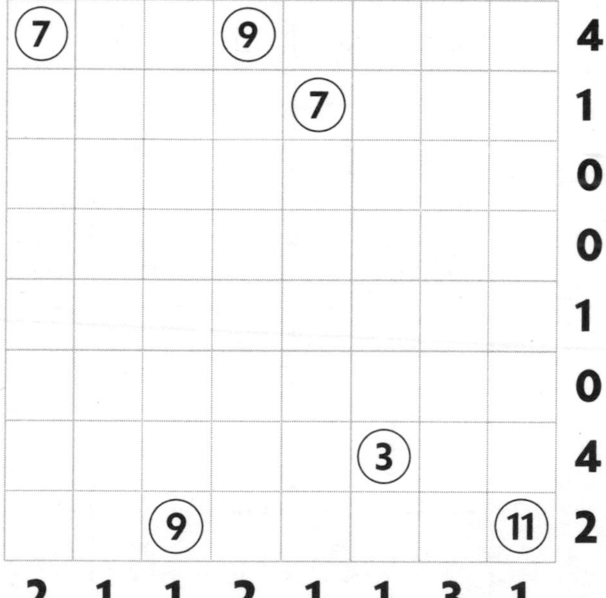

SOLUTION PAGE 153

MEDIUM

					(4)			3
								3
			(2)					1
	(7)							1
(5)							(9)	2
								2
		(5)						1
(8)								1
2	2	3	1	1	1	3	1	

SOLUTION PAGE 153

HARD

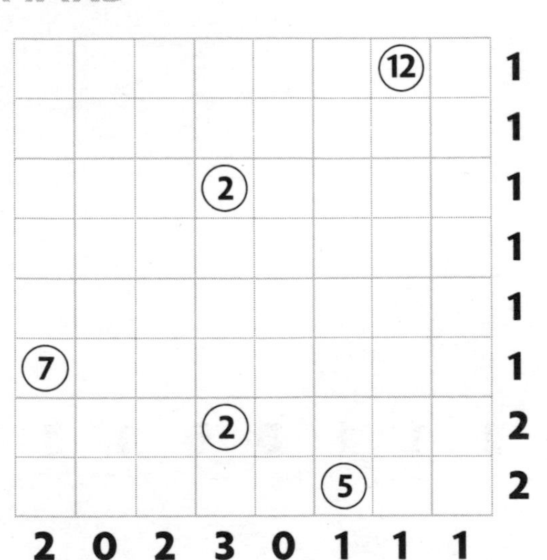

SOLUTION PAGE 154

ELBOW ROOM

Draw a horizontal and vertical line from each circled number in an "L" shape. The circled number equates to the number of cells that the lines travel through in total, and the numbers outside of the grid represent the number of lines that finish in each respective row and column. The lines can never intersect.

MEDIUM

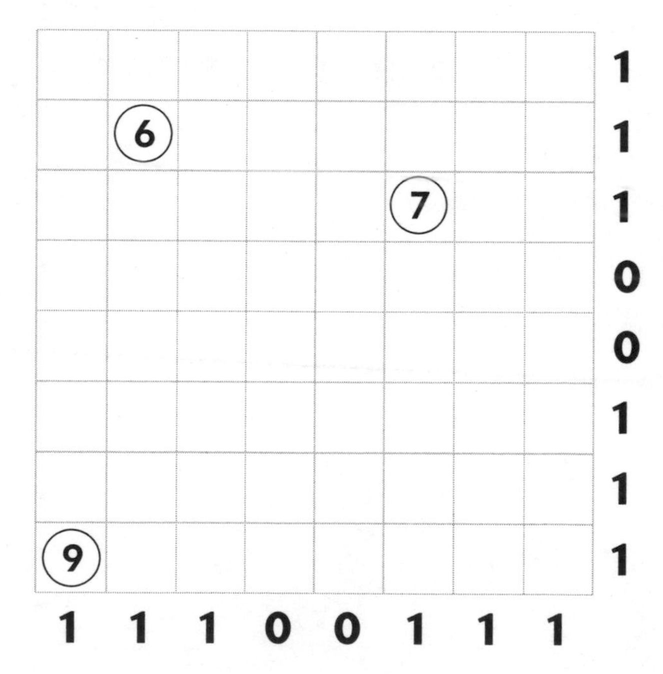

SOLUTION PAGE 154

BAR CODE

Add horizontal and vertical bars – no longer than the length of a single cell – to the grid in such a way that no two bars touch. The numbers outside of the grid equate to the number of bars that appear consecutively in their respective row and column. Where two or more numbers are given, at least one row or column must separate the groups of bars.

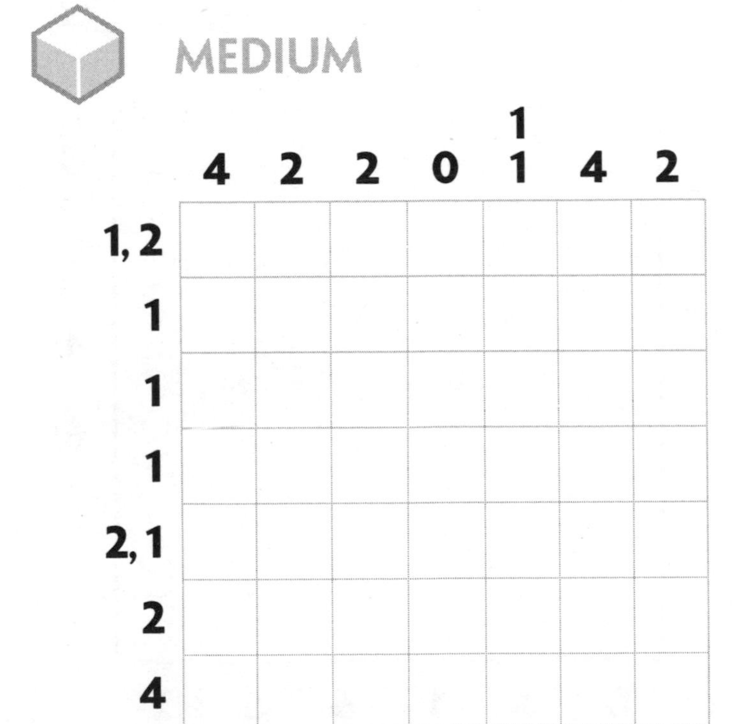

SOLUTION PAGE 154

CANDIES

Place numbers from 1 to 6 into the grid so that no number appears more than once in the same row or column. The numbers outside the grid equate to the sum of the numbers in their respective row or column. The numbers in each row must increase from left to right, and in each column must increase from top to bottom.

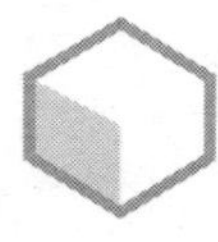

EASY

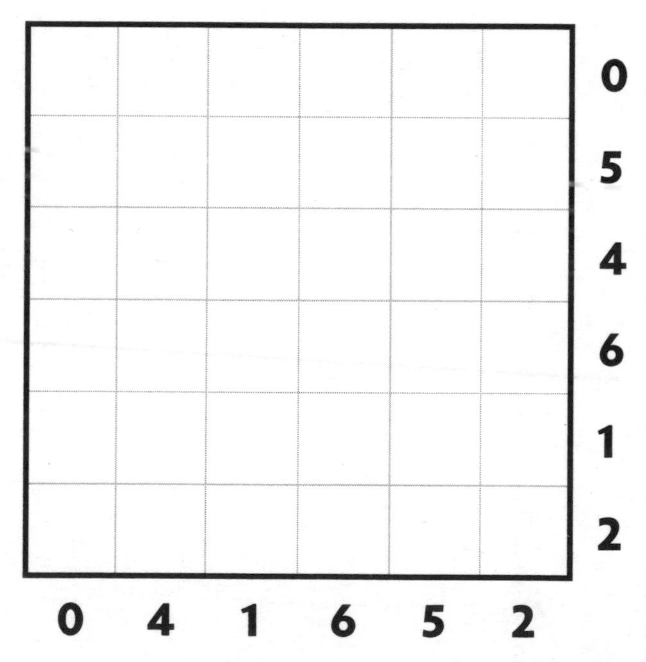

SOLUTION PAGE 155

MEDIUM

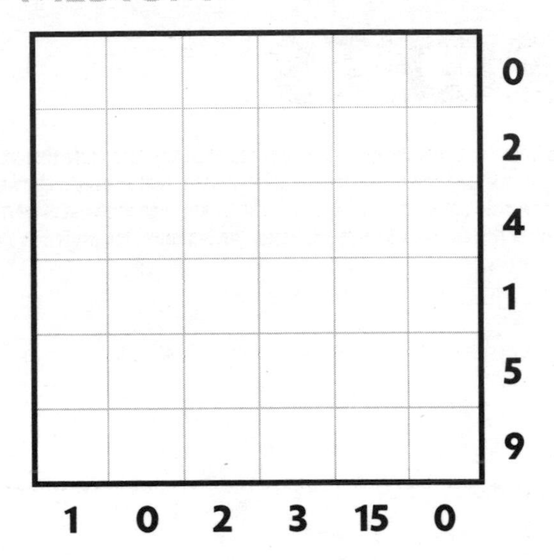

SOLUTION PAGE 155

HARD

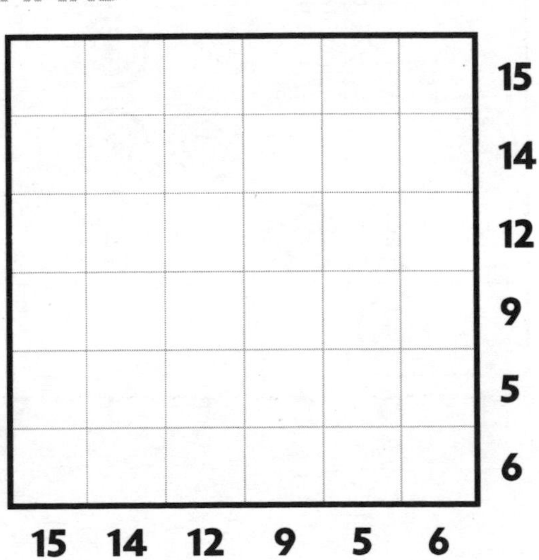

SOLUTION PAGE 155

TARGETS

Place arrows into the cells in the grid to complete the Targets puzzle. The numbers outside of the grid equate to numbers of arrows located in their respective row and column. The arrows can point up, down, left, right or in any diagonal and must be placed so that every target has an arrow heading towards the bullseye. No arrow can shoot through another arrow.

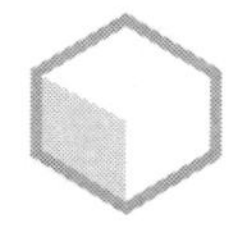

EASY

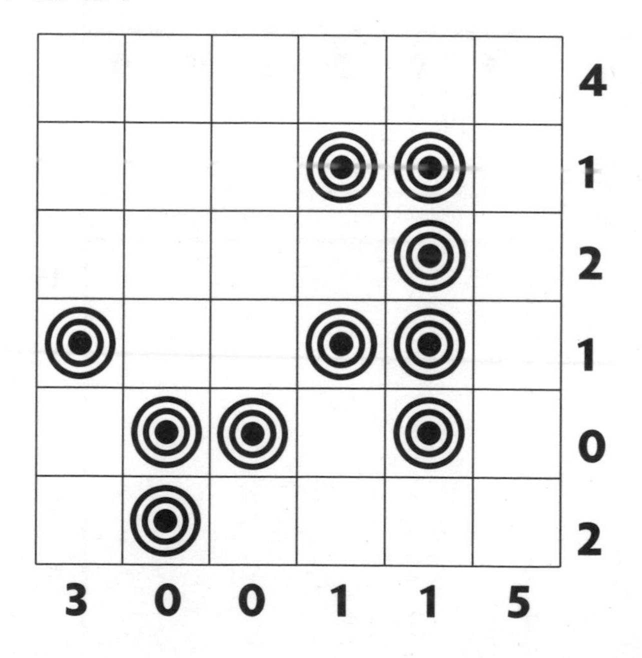

SOLUTION PAGE 156

MEDIUM

		◎		◎		2
◎			◎			0
◎						2
			◎		◎	2
◎				◎		0
					◎	4
2	1	2	1	2	2	

SOLUTION PAGE 156

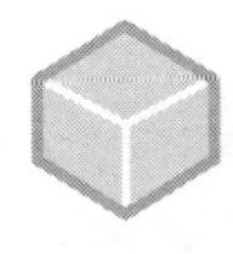

HARD

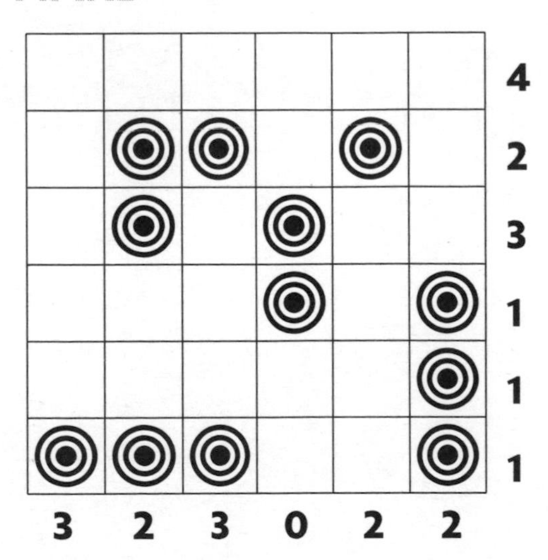

SOLUTION PAGE 156

BAR CODE

Add horizontal and vertical bars – no longer than the length of a single cell – to the grid in such a way that no two bars touch. The numbers outside of the grid equate to the number of bars that appear consecutively in their respective row and column. Where two or more numbers are given, at least one row or column must separate the groups of bars.

EASY

	2	1	1 1	3	1	2
1, 2						
0						
1						
0						
1, 2						
1, 2, 1						

SOLUTION PAGE 157

MEDIUM

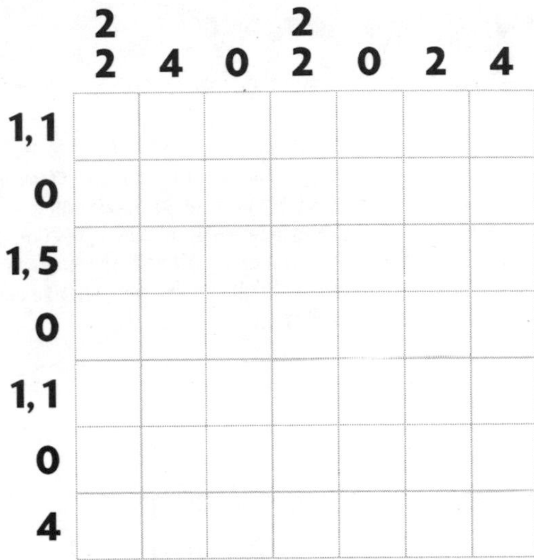

SOLUTION PAGE 157

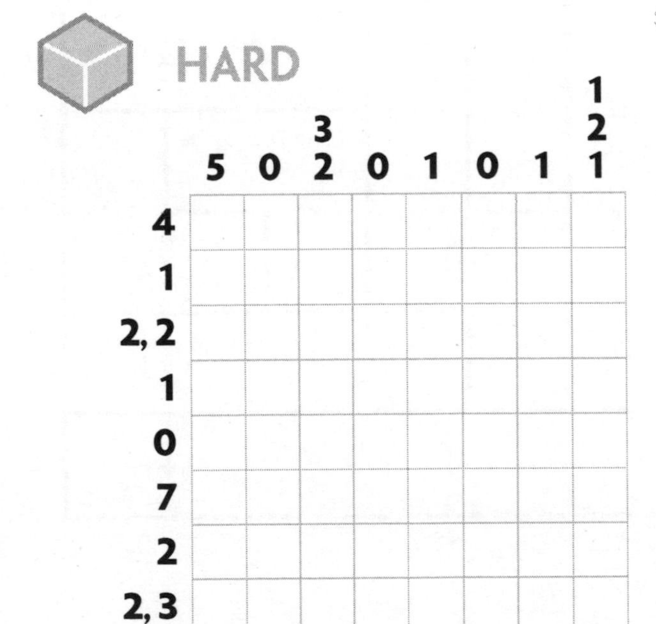

HARD

SOLUTION PAGE 157

MATH BOX

Place numbers from 1 to 6 (or 7 in the case of the Hard puzzle) into the grid so that no two numbers appear in the same row or column. Each bold-lined region contains mathematical operations – these must be calculated to solve the puzzle and the questions within – and arrows. The double arrows indicate the direction that the operations must be calculated in, and also represent an equals sign. The single arrows indicate where two digits are joined to create a two-digit number. You may also need to use brackets to complete some of the calculations.

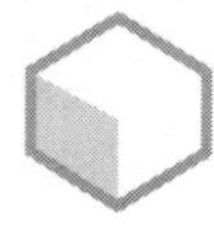

EASY

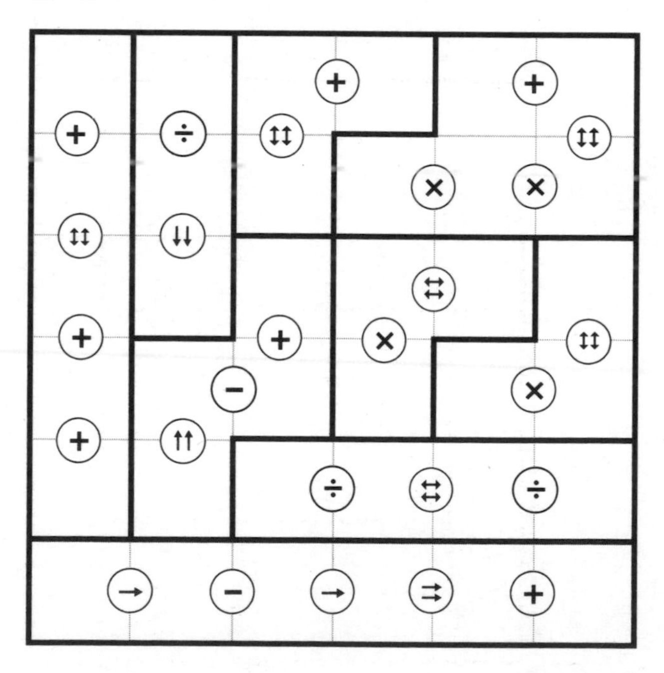

SOLUTION PAGE 158

MEDIUM

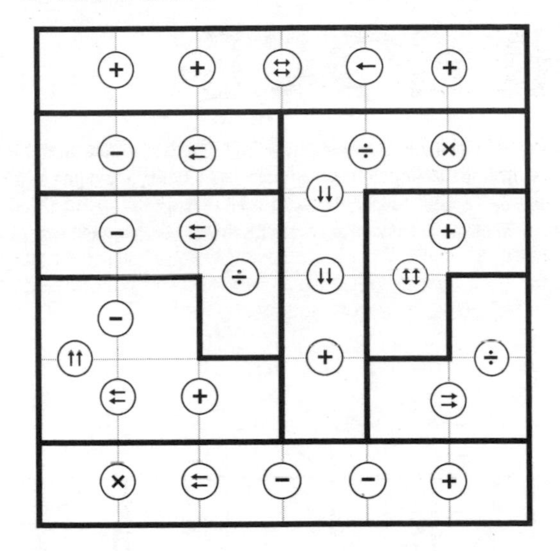

SOLUTION PAGE 158

HARD

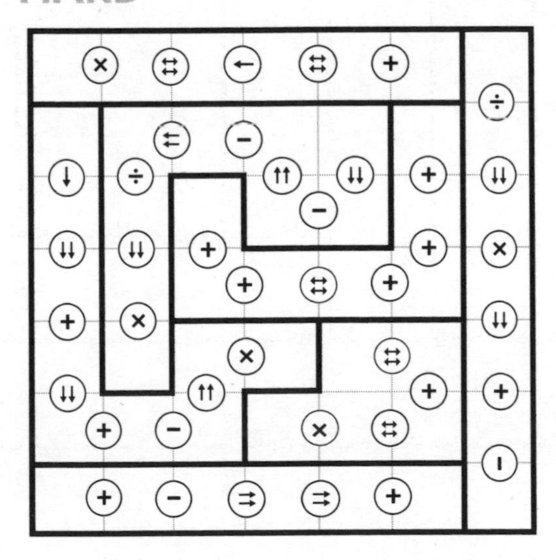

SOLUTION PAGE 158

BAR CODE

Add horizontal and vertical bars – no longer than the length of a single cell – to the grid in such a way that no two bars touch. The numbers outside of the grid equate to the number of bars that appear consecutively in their respective row and column. Where two or more numbers are given, at least one row or column must separate the groups of bars.

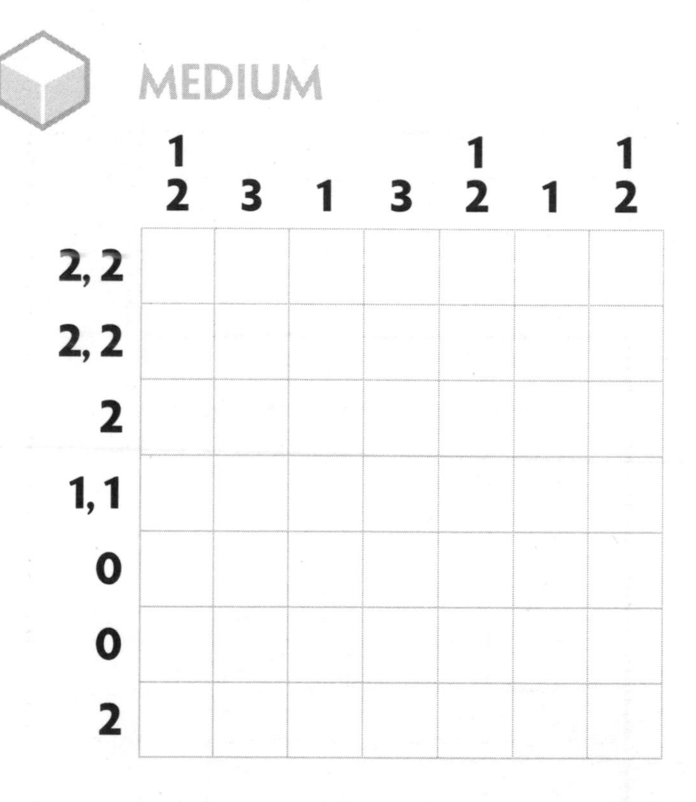

SOLUTION PAGE 159

MATH BOX

Place numbers from 1 to 6 into the grid so that no two numbers appear in the same row or column. Each bold-lined region contains mathematical operations – these must be calculated to solve the puzzle and the questions within – and arrows. The double arrows indicate the direction that the operations must be calculated in, and also represent an equals sign. The single arrows indicate where two digits are joined to create a two-digit number. You may also need to use brackets to complete some of the calculations.

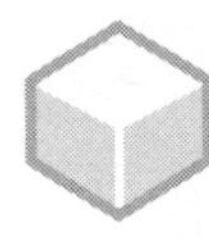

MEDIUM

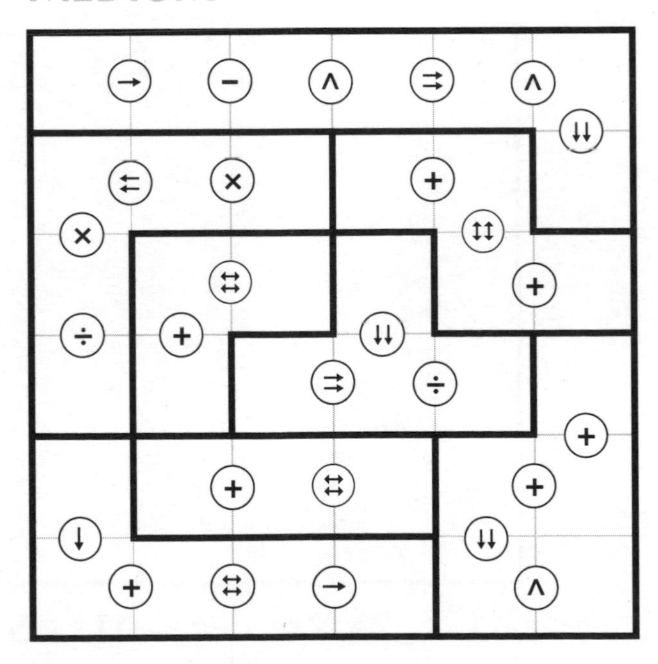

SOLUTION PAGE 159

CANDIES

Place numbers from 1 to 6 into the grid so that no number appears more than once in the same row or column. The numbers outside the grid equate to the sum of the numbers in their respective row or column. The numbers in each row must increase from left to right, and in each column must increase from top to bottom.

MEDIUM

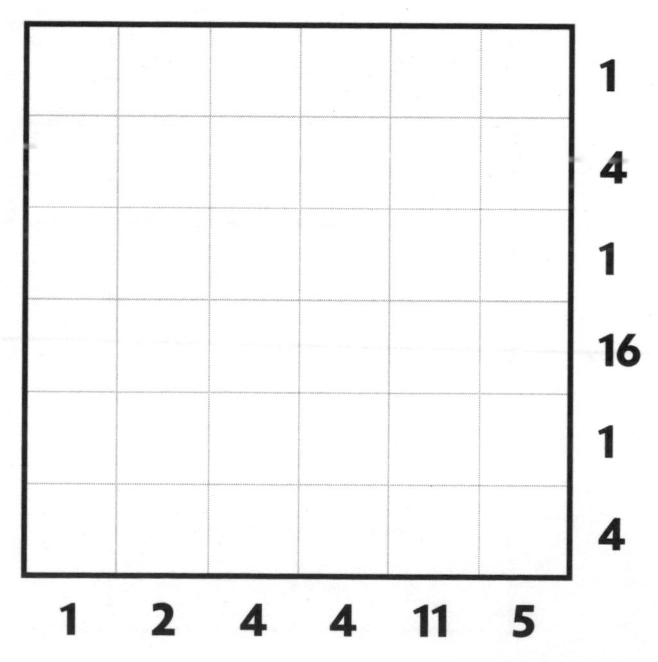

SOLUTION PAGE 159

TARGETS

Place arrows into the cells in the grid to complete the Targets puzzle. The numbers outside of the grid equate to numbers of arrows located in their respective row and column. The arrows can point up, down, left, right or in any diagonal and must be placed so that every target has an arrow heading towards the bullseye. No arrow can shoot through another arrow.

MEDIUM

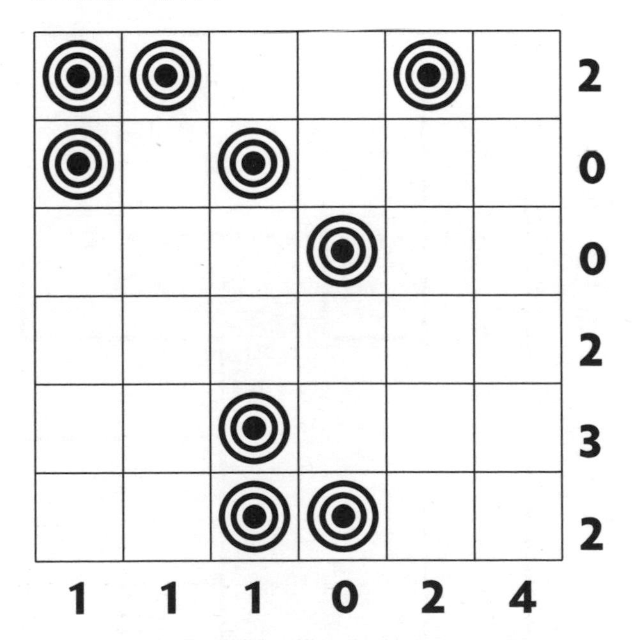

SOLUTION PAGE 160

MATH BOX

Place numbers from 1 to 6 (or 7 in the case of the Hard puzzle) into the grid so that no two numbers appear in the same row or column. Each bold-lined region contains mathematical operations – these must be calculated to solve the puzzle and the questions within – and arrows. The double arrows indicate the direction that the operations must be calculated in, and also represent an equals sign. The single arrows indicate where two digits are joined to create a two-digit number. You may also need to use brackets to complete some of the calculations.

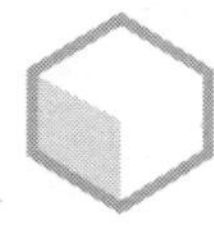

EASY

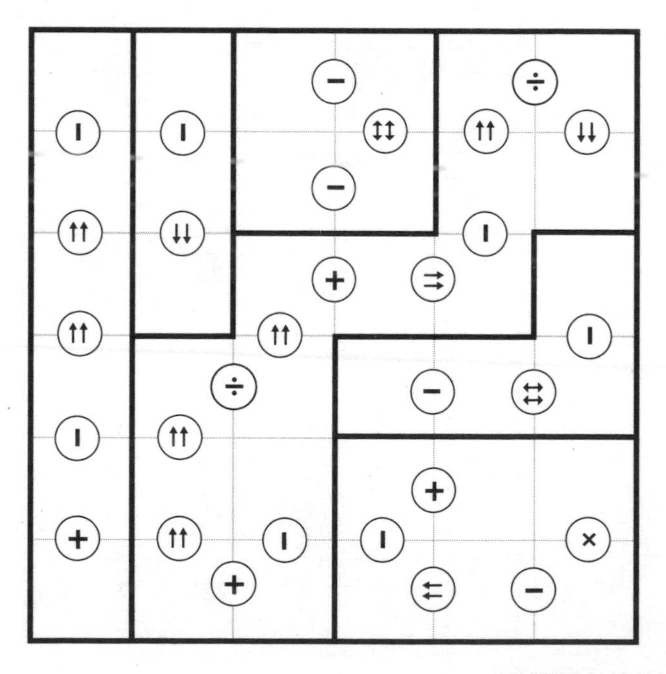

SOLUTION PAGE 160

MEDIUM

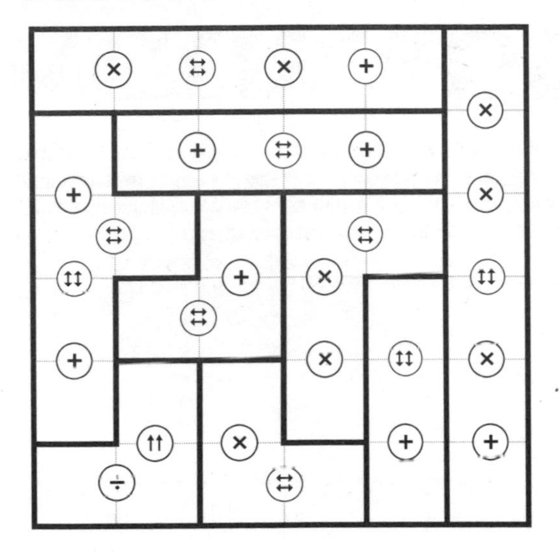

SOLUTION PAGE 160

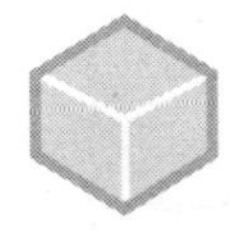

HARD

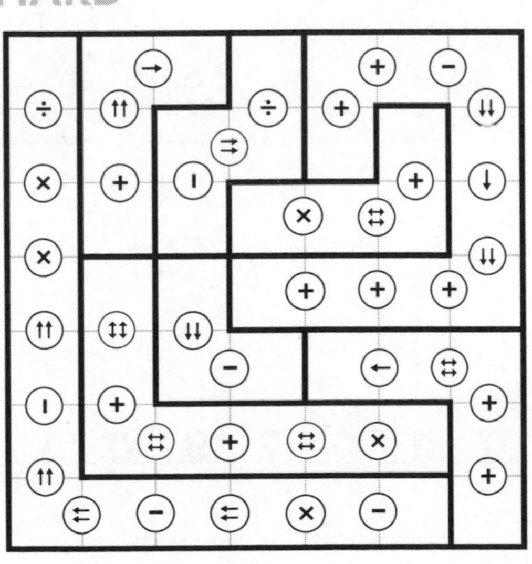

SOLUTION PAGE 161

ELBOW ROOM

Draw a horizontal and vertical line from each circled number in an "L" shape. The circled number equates to the number of cells that the lines travel through in total, and the numbers outside of the grid represent the number of lines that finish in each respective row and column. The lines can never intersect.

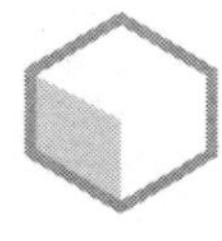

EASY

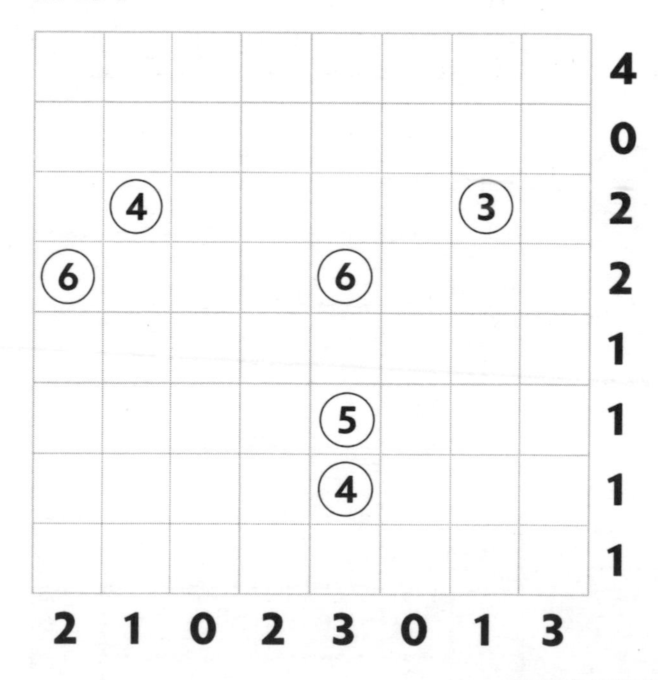

SOLUTION PAGE 161

MEDIUM

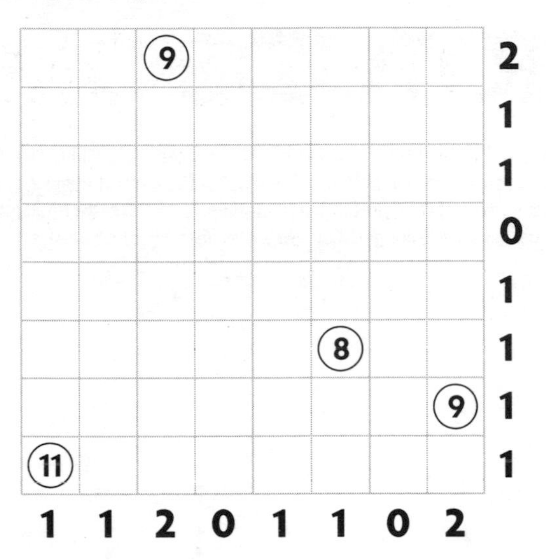

SOLUTION PAGE 161

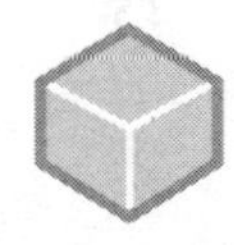

HARD

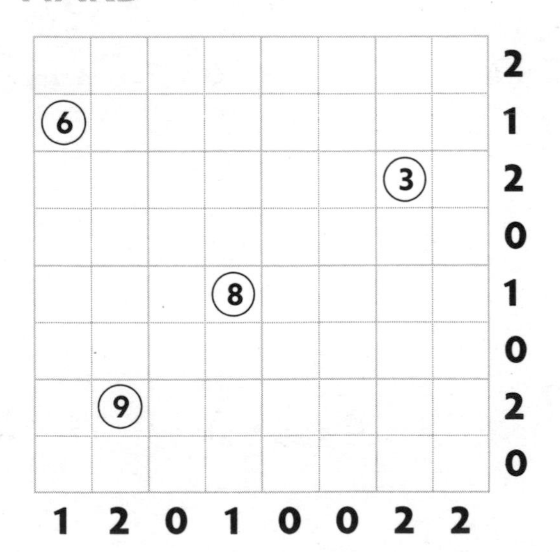

SOLUTION PAGE 162

BAR CODE

Add horizontal and vertical bars – no longer than the length of a single cell – to the grid in such a way that no two bars touch. The numbers outside of the grid equate to the number of bars that appear consecutively in their respective row and column. Where two or more numbers are given, at least one row or column must separate the groups of bars.

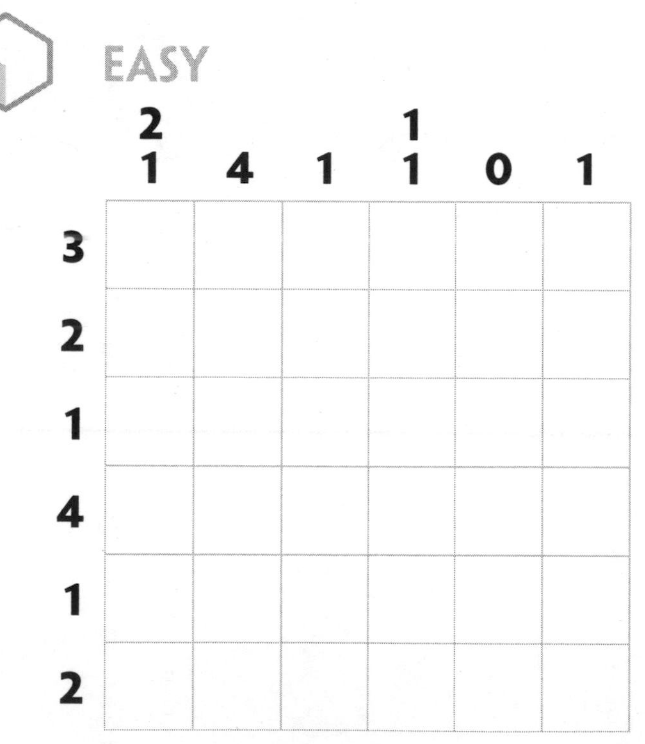

SOLUTION PAGE 162

MEDIUM

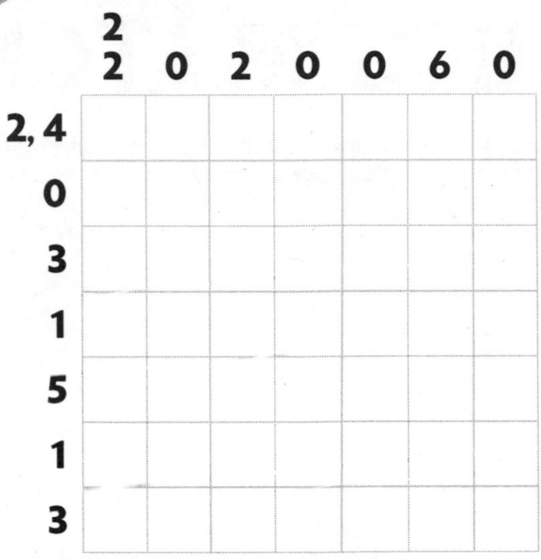

SOLUTION PAGE 162

HARD

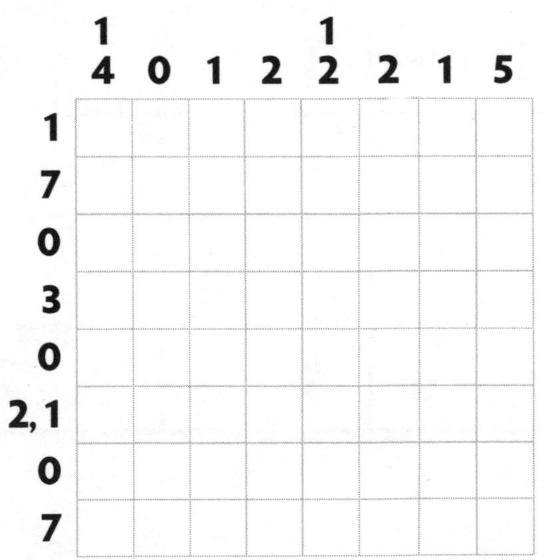

SOLUTION PAGE 163

BOXING MATCH

Place numbers from 1 to 9 into the grid so that the numbers in each bold-lined region are consecutive, and so that every 3x3 grid of squares in the entire puzzle grid sum to the same total.

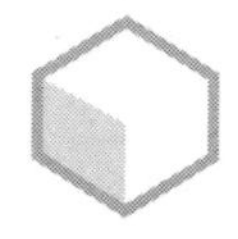

EASY

1		6	2		7
				4	
4	5	3			1
3		1		4	2
			5		
	3	4			2

SOLUTION PAGE 163

MEDIUM

		2		3	
	6		8	7	5
		7			5
7	5	2		4	
	8		8		
4		5			3

SOLUTION PAGE 163

HARD

6		7			5
		4		4	
5					5
		5		8	
			4	7	
6	8				2

SOLUTION PAGE 164

TARGETS

Place arrows into the cells in the grid to complete the Targets puzzle. The numbers outside of the grid equate to numbers of arrows located in their respective row and column. The arrows can point up, down, left, right or in any diagonal and must be placed so that every target has an arrow heading towards the bullseye. No arrow can shoot through another arrow.

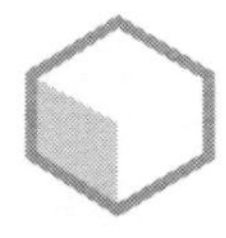

EASY

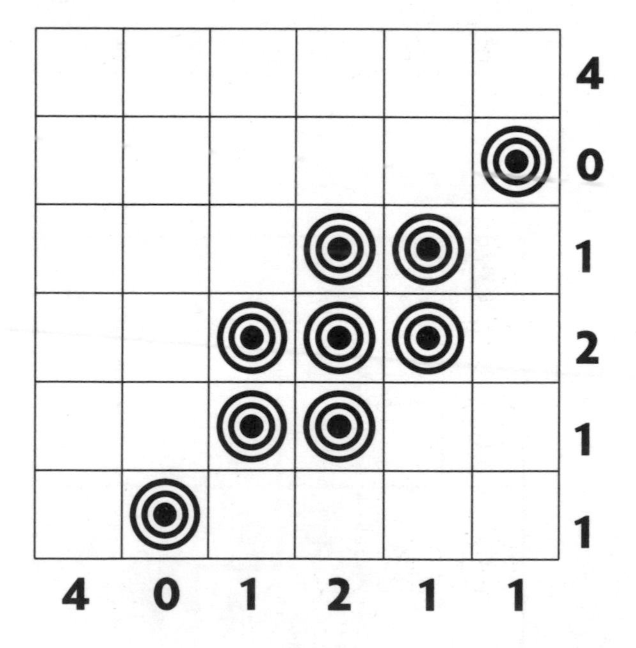

SOLUTION PAGE 164

MEDIUM

	◎					3
	◎					2
◎	◎				◎	0
◎	◎				◎	1
						1
◎	◎					3
2	0	1	2	1	4	

SOLUTION PAGE 164

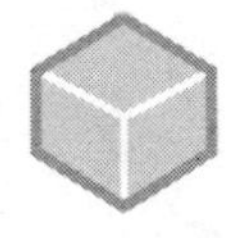

HARD

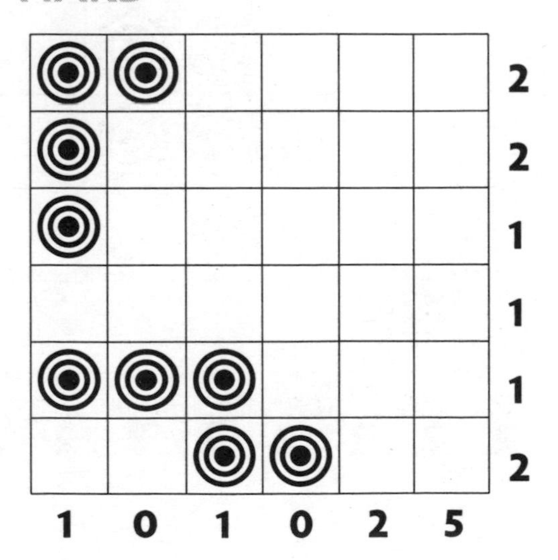

SOLUTION PAGE 165

ELBOW ROOM

Draw a horizontal and vertical line from each circled number in an "L" shape. The circled number equates to the number of cells that the lines travel through in total, and the numbers outside of the grid represent the number of lines that finish in each respective row and column. The lines can never intersect.

MEDIUM

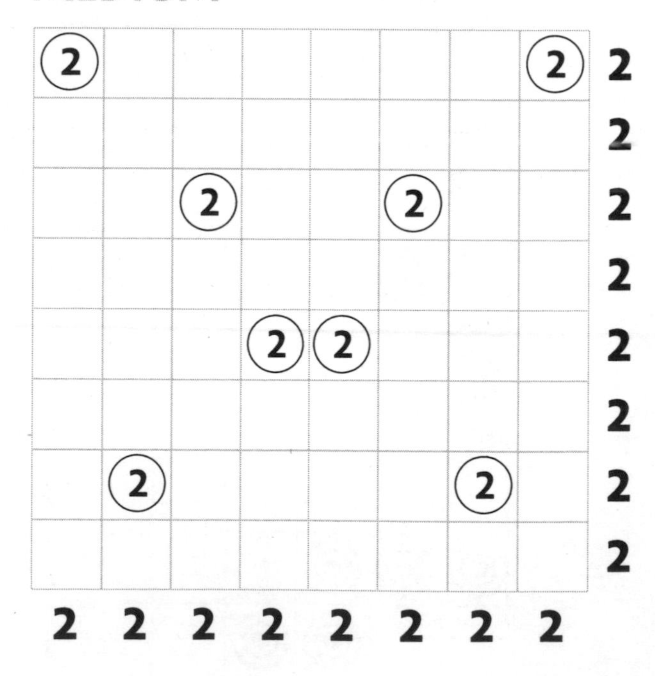

SOLUTION PAGE 165

BOXING MATCH

Place numbers from 1 to 9 into the grid so that the numbers in each bold-lined region are consecutive, and so that every 3x3 grid of squares in the entire puzzle grid sum to the same total.

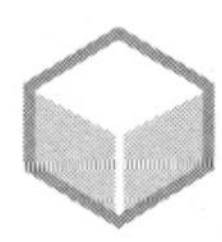

MEDIUM

	5			4	6
4		4			
		8			7
	5		6		
			3	4	
3		6			5

SOLUTION PAGE 165

CANDIES

Place numbers from 1 to 6 into the grid so that no number appears more than once in the same row or column. The numbers outside the grid equate to the sum of the numbers in their respective row or column. The numbers in each row must increase from left to right, and in each column must increase from top to bottom.

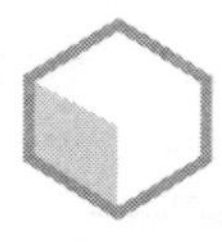

EASY

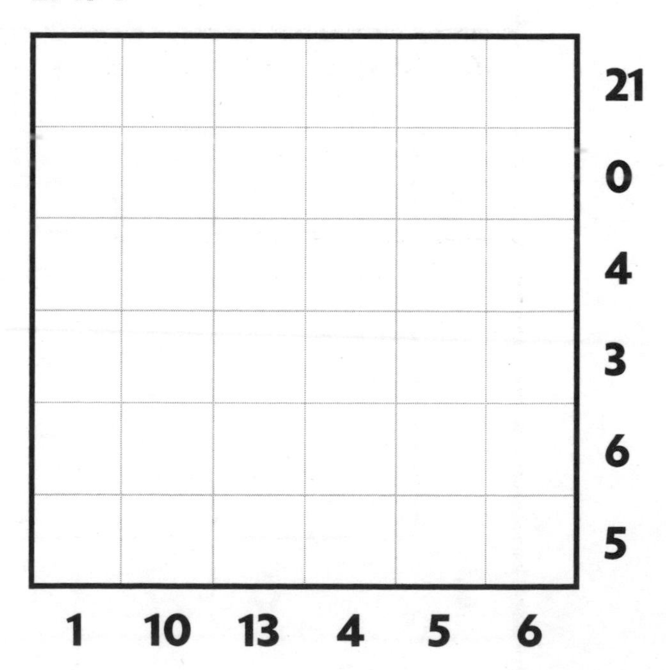

SOLUTION PAGE 166

MEDIUM

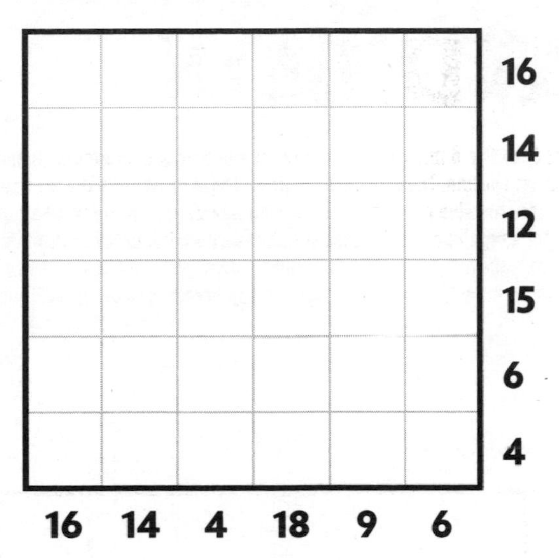

SOLUTION PAGE 166

HARD

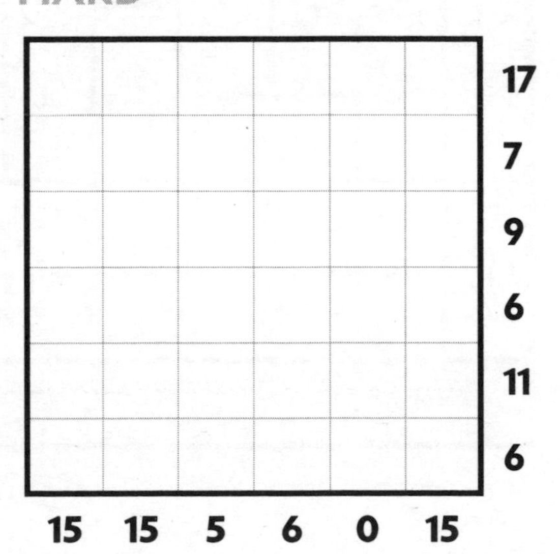

SOLUTION PAGE 166

MATH BOX

Place numbers from 1 to 7 into the grid so that no two numbers appear in the same row or column. Each bold-lined region contains mathematical operations – these must be calculated to solve the puzzle and the questions within – and arrows. The double arrows indicate the direction that the operations must be calculated in, and also represent an equals sign. The single arrows indicate where two digits are joined to create a two-digit number. You may also need to use brackets to complete some of the calculations.

MEDIUM

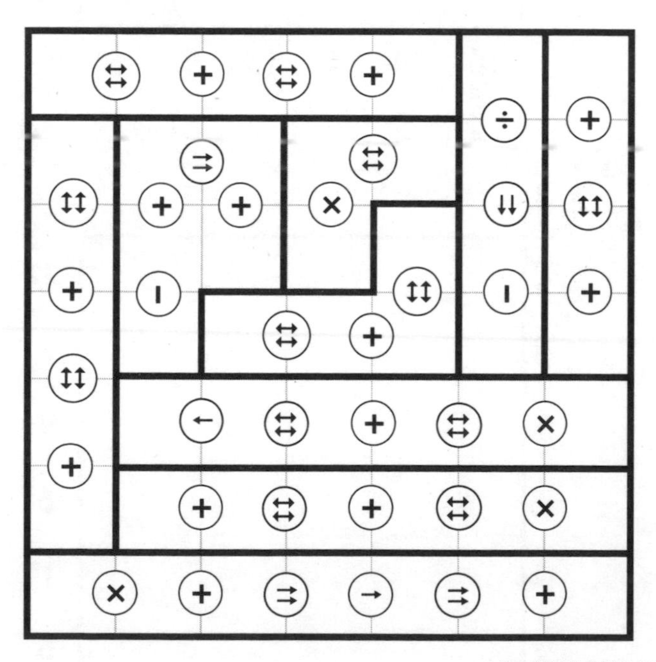

SOLUTION PAGE 167

BAR CODE

Add horizontal and vertical bars – no longer than the length of a single cell – to the grid in such a way that no two bars touch. The numbers outside of the grid equate to the number of bars that appear consecutively in their respective row and column. Where two or more numbers are given, at least one row or column must separate the groups of bars.

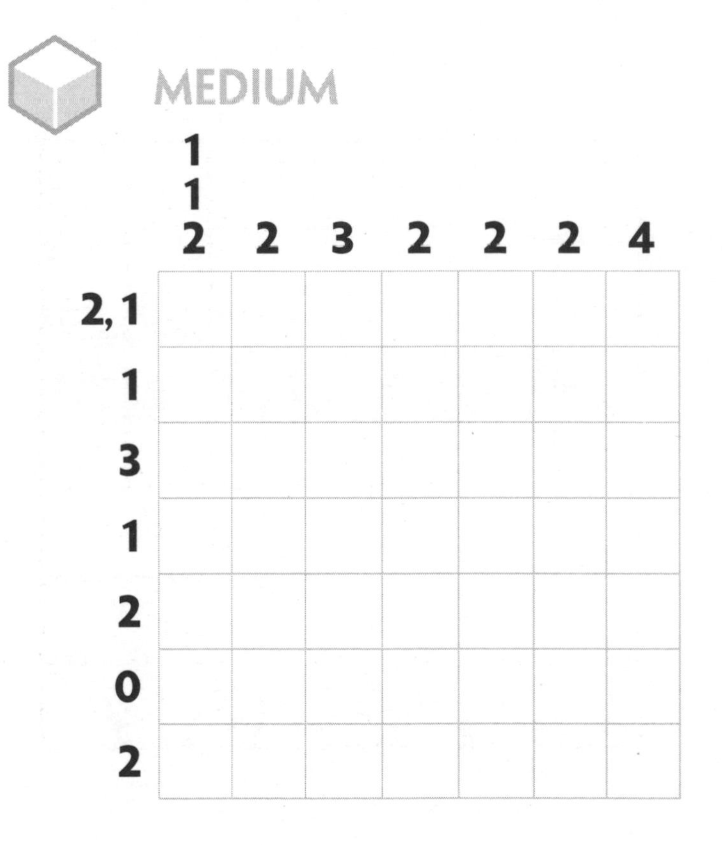

SOLUTION PAGE 167

ELBOW ROOM

Draw a horizontal and vertical line from each circled number in an "L" shape. The circled number equates to the number of cells that the lines travel through in total, and the numbers outside of the grid represent the number of lines that finish in each respective row and column. The lines can never intersect.

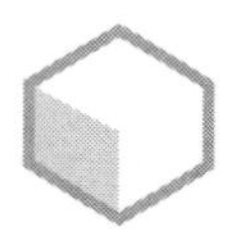

EASY

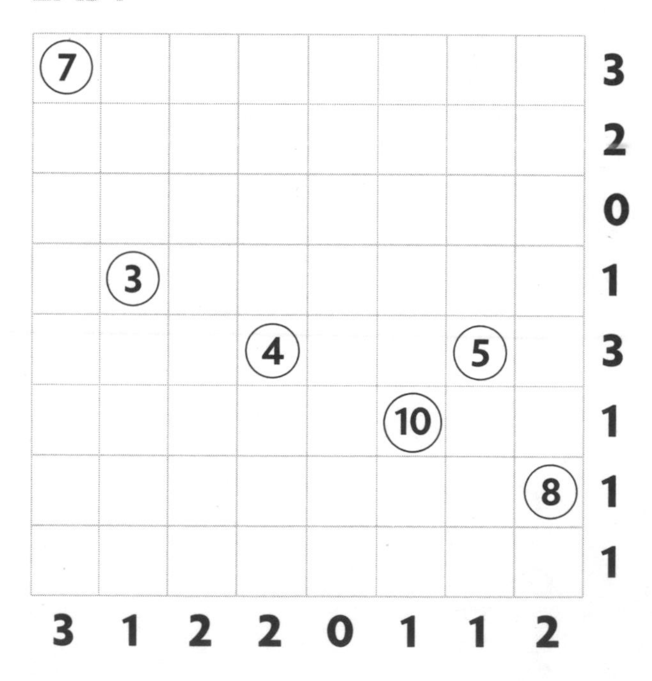

SOLUTION PAGE 167

MEDIUM

			7		8			2
		6						2
								2
								0
								0
						5		3
6								2
				8				1
2	2	2	1	1	1	1	2	

SOLUTION PAGE 168

HARD

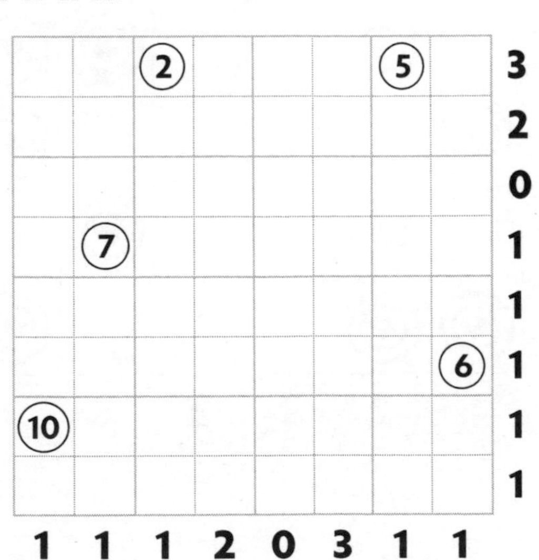

		2				5		3
								2
								0
	7							1
								1
							6	1
10								1
								1
1	1	1	2	0	3	1	1	

SOLUTION PAGE 168

TARGETS

Place arrows into the cells in the grid to complete the Targets puzzle. The numbers outside of the grid equate to numbers of arrows located in their respective row and column. The arrows can point up, down, left, right or in any diagonal and must be placed so that every target has an arrow heading towards the bullseye. No arrow can shoot through another arrow.

MEDIUM

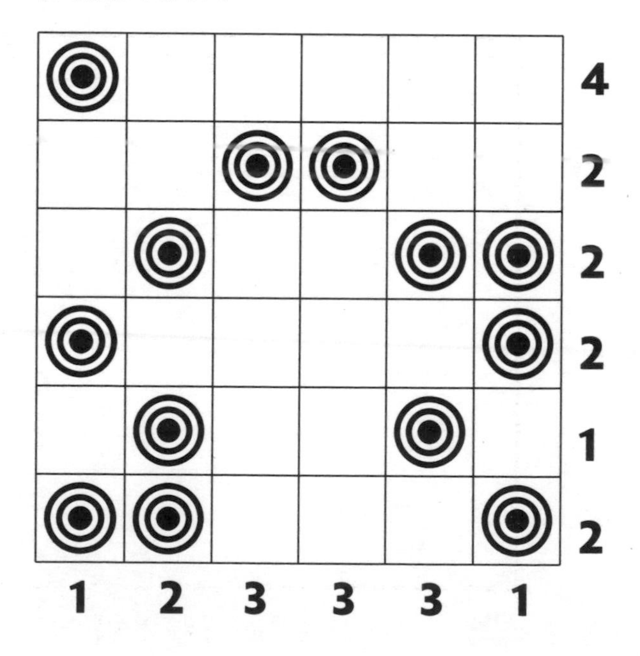

SOLUTION PAGE 168

CANDIES

Place numbers from 1 to 6 into the grid so that no number appears more than once in the same row or column. The numbers outside the grid equate to the sum of the numbers in their respective row or column. The numbers in each row must increase from left to right, and in each column must increase from top to bottom.

HARD

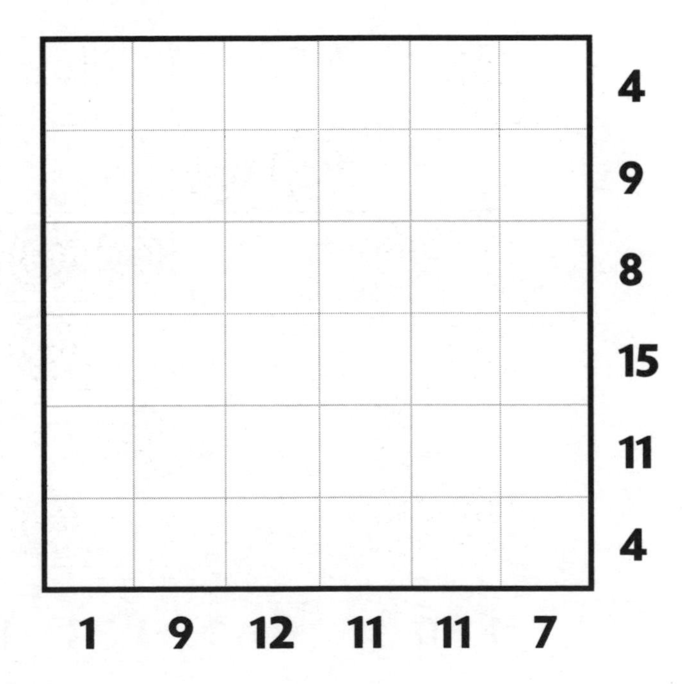

SOLUTION PAGE 169

ELBOW ROOM

Draw a horizontal and vertical line from each circled number in an "L" shape. The circled number equates to the number of cells that the lines travel through in total, and the numbers outside of the grid represent the number of lines that finish in each respective row and column. The lines can never intersect.

HARD

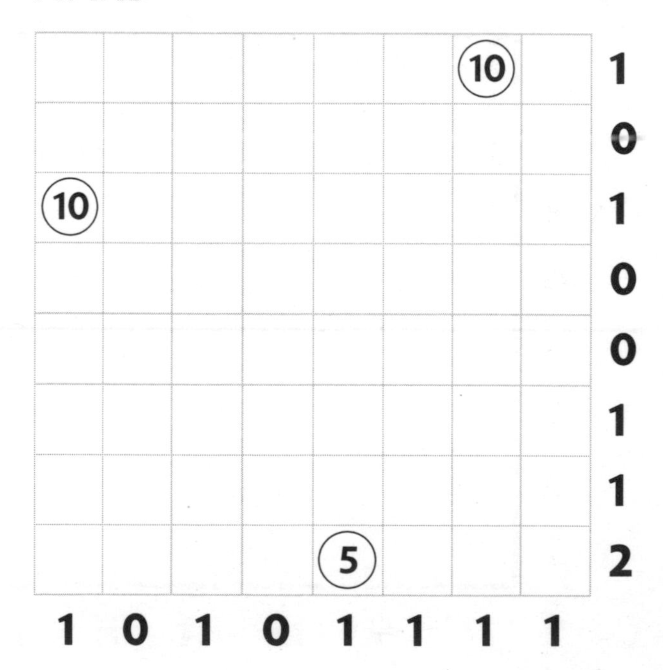

SOLUTION PAGE 169

BAR CODE

Add horizontal and vertical bars – no longer than the length of a single cell – to the grid in such a way that no two bars touch. The numbers outside of the grid equate to the number of bars that appear consecutively in their respective row and column. Where two or more numbers are given, at least one row or column must separate the groups of bars.

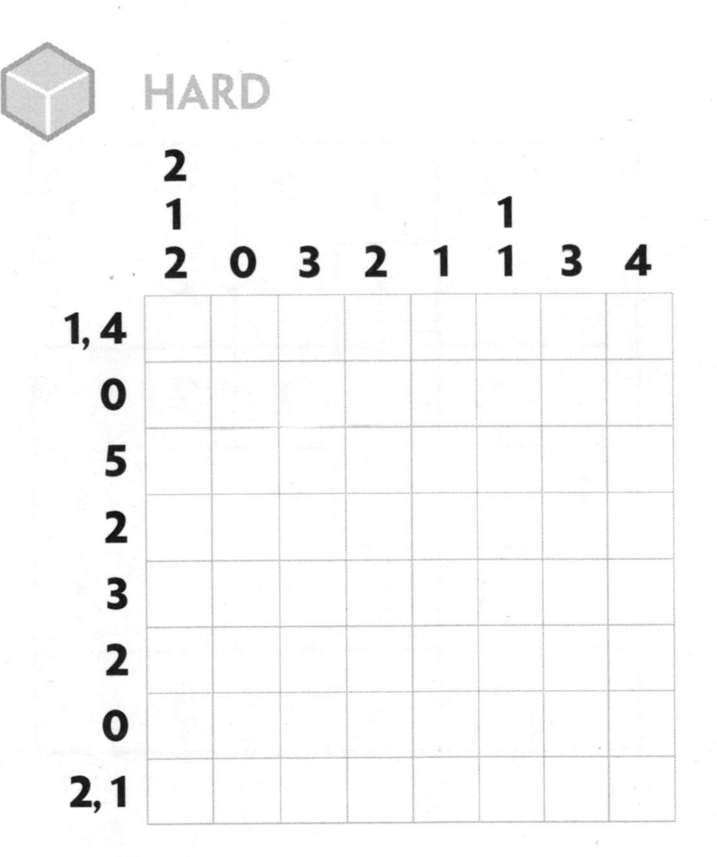

SOLUTION PAGE 169

BOXING MATCH

Place numbers from 1 to 9 into the grid so that the numbers in each bold-lined region are consecutive, and so that every 3x3 grid of squares in the entire puzzle grid sum to the same total.

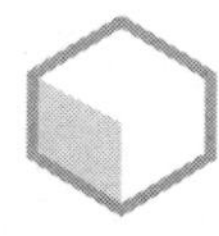

EASY

	4	6	8		3
		3		6	
	8		1	7	
4			9		1
	5	2			4
				5	

SOLUTION PAGE 170

MEDIUM

3	4				4
			3		
6	5	2			7
4				5	4
	6		3		
4		3			8

SOLUTION PAGE 170

HARD

6		8			5
			3	4	
1		3			
				4	3
	3		2	5	
	3				4

SOLUTION PAGE 170

MATH BOX

Place numbers from 1 to 6 (or 7 in the case of the Hard puzzle) into the grid so that no two numbers appear in the same row or column. Each bold-lined region contains mathematical operations – these must be calculated to solve the puzzle and the questions within – and arrows. The double arrows indicate the direction that the operations must be calculated in, and also represent an equals sign. The single arrows indicate where two digits are joined to create a two-digit number. You may also need to use brackets to complete some of the calculations.

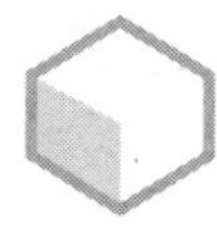

EASY

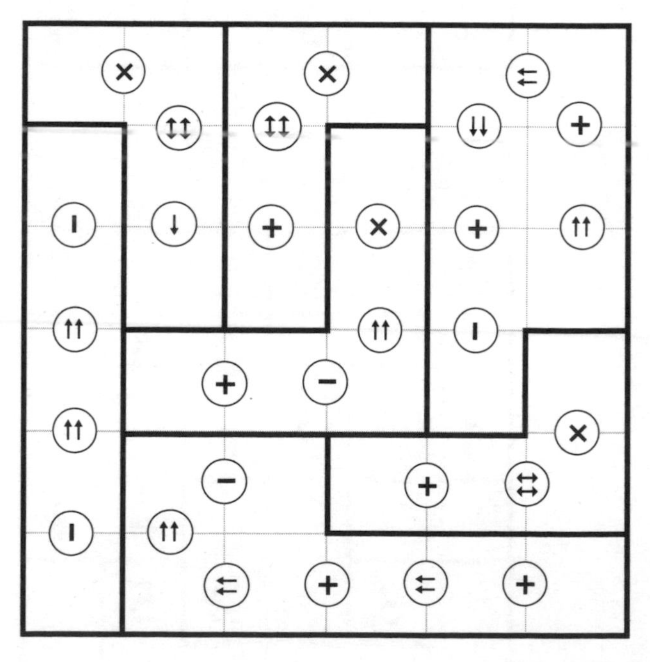

SOLUTION PAGE 171

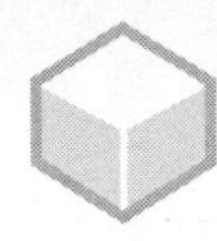

MEDIUM

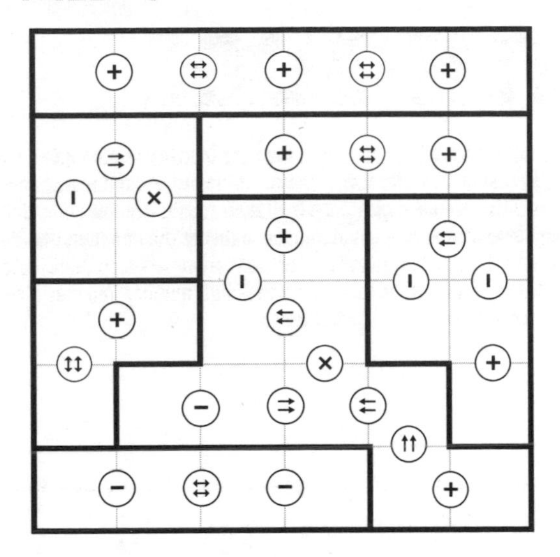

SOLUTION PAGE 171

HARD

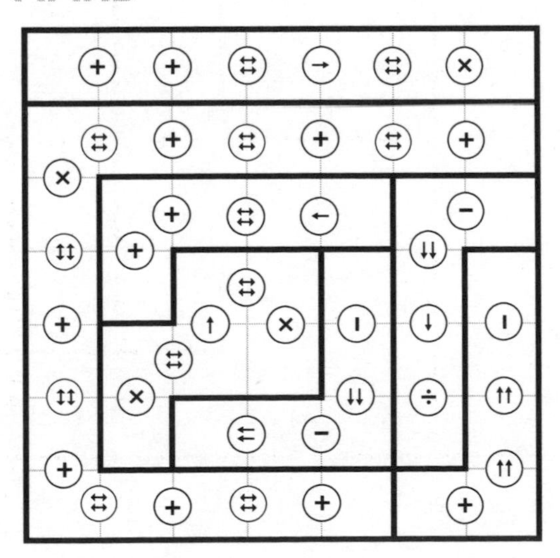

SOLUTION PAGE 171

BAR CODE

Add horizontal and vertical bars – no longer than the length of a single cell – to the grid in such a way that no two bars touch. The numbers outside of the grid equate to the number of bars that appear consecutively in their respective row and column. Where two or more numbers are given, at least one row or column must separate the groups of bars.

EASY

SOLUTION PAGE 172

MEDIUM

	2 2	0	6	0	4	0	3 1
6							
0							
0							
2							
2							
2							
2							

SOLUTION PAGE 172

HARD

	2 2	3	0	2 3	2	1 2	0	4 1
1, 2								
0								
4, 1								
0								
1, 2								
2								
0								
3, 2								

SOLUTION PAGE 172

CANDIES

Place numbers from 1 to 6 into the grid so that no number appears more than once in the same row or column. The numbers outside the grid equate to the sum of the numbers in their respective row or column. The numbers in each row must increase from left to right, and in each column must increase from top to bottom.

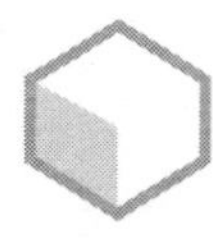

EASY

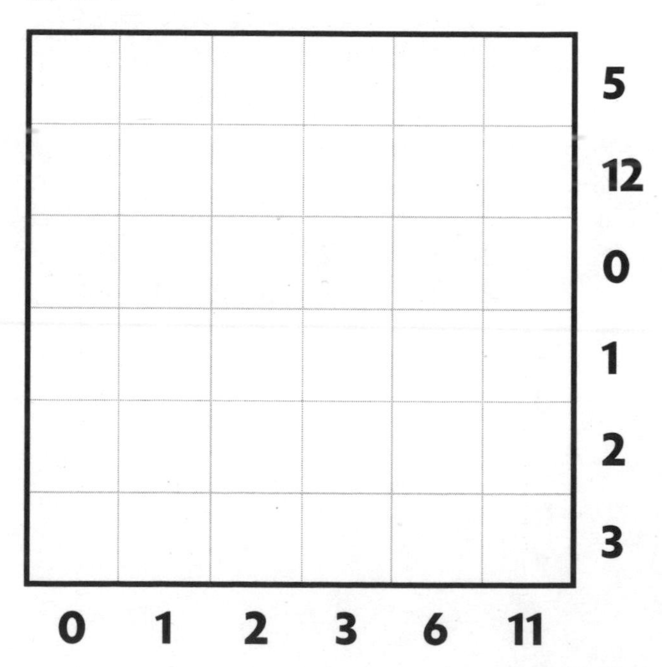

SOLUTION PAGE 173

MEDIUM

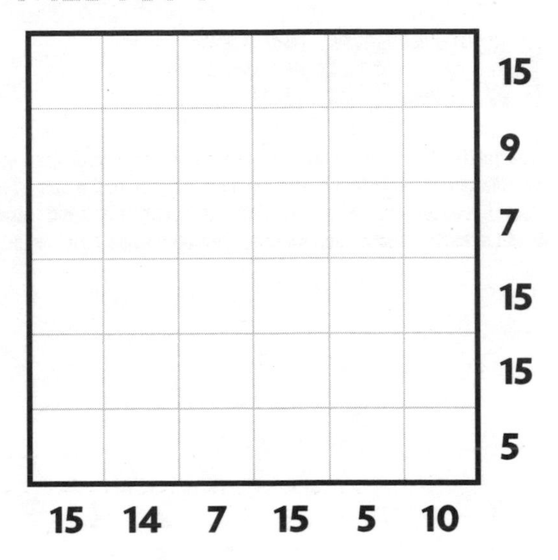

SOLUTION PAGE 173

HARD

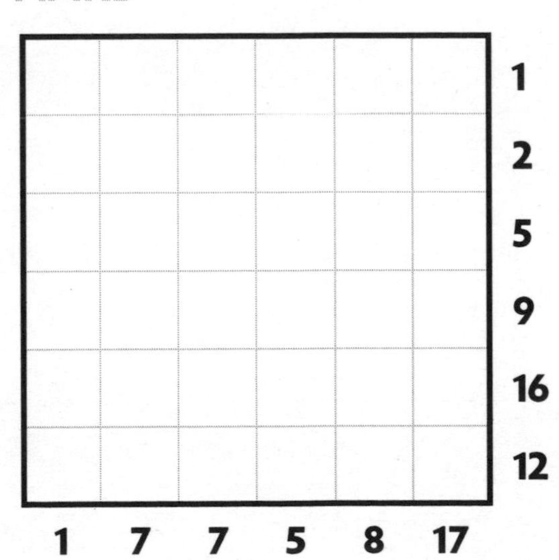

SOLUTION PAGE 173

BAR CODE

Add horizontal and vertical bars – no longer than the length of a single cell – to the grid in such a way that no two bars touch. The numbers outside of the grid equate to the number of bars that appear consecutively in their respective row and column. Where two or more numbers are given, at least one row or column must separate the groups of bars.

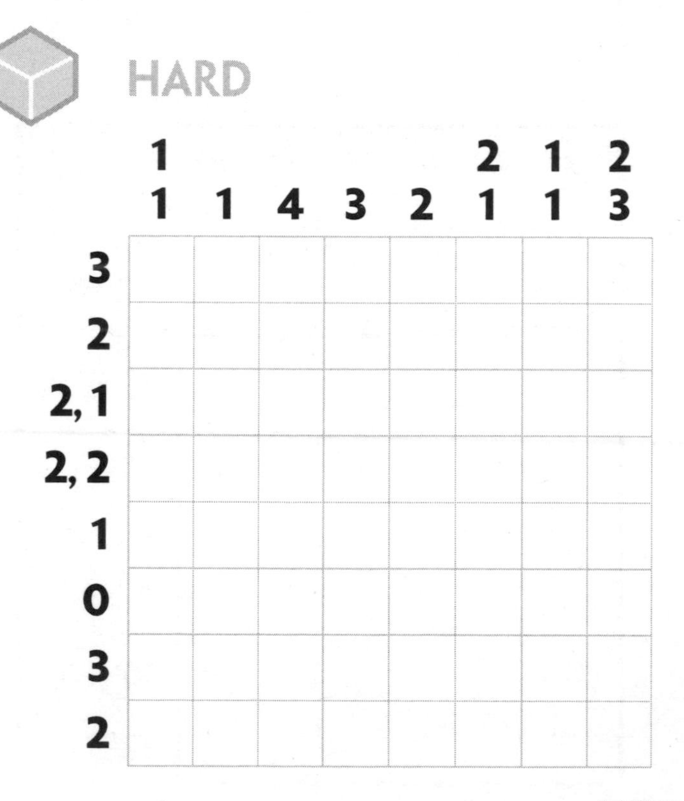

SOLUTION PAGE 174

BOXING MATCH

Place numbers from 1 to 9 into the grid so that the numbers in each bold-lined region are consecutive, and so that every 3x3 grid of squares in the entire puzzle grid sum to the same total.

HARD

4			2		5
		3			4
8					
	5			3	
		6		3	
7			8		8

SOLUTION PAGE 174

TARGETS

Place arrows into the cells in the grid to complete the Targets puzzle. The numbers outside of the grid equate to numbers of arrows located in their respective row and column. The arrows can point up, down, left, right or in any diagonal and must be placed so that every target has an arrow heading towards the bullseye. No arrow can shoot through another arrow.

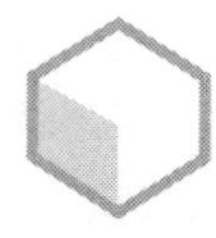

EASY

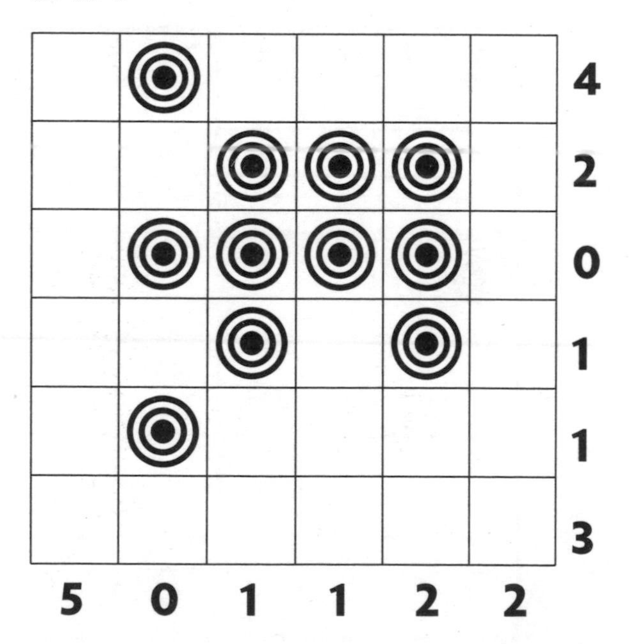

SOLUTION PAGE 174

MEDIUM

◎		◎			◎	0
		◎	◎			1
			◎	◎		1
					◎	1
						1
						4
4	1	0	1	1	1	

SOLUTION PAGE 175

HARD

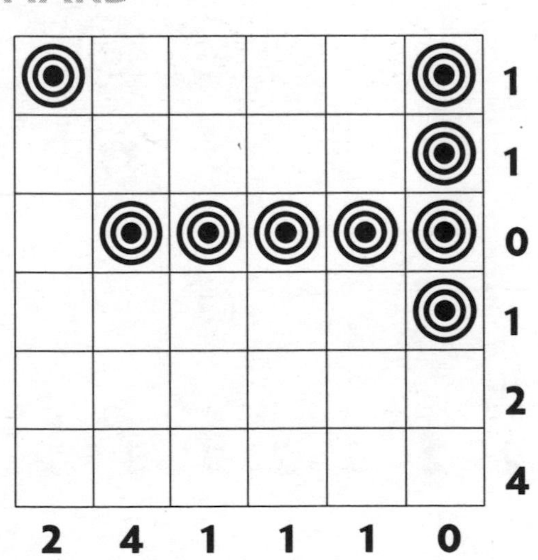

SOLUTION PAGE 175

ELBOW ROOM

Draw a horizontal and vertical line from each circled number in an "L" shape. The circled number equates to the number of cells that the lines travel through in total, and the numbers outside of the grid represent the number of lines that finish in each respective row and column. The lines can never intersect.

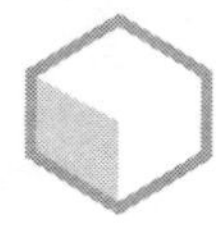

EASY

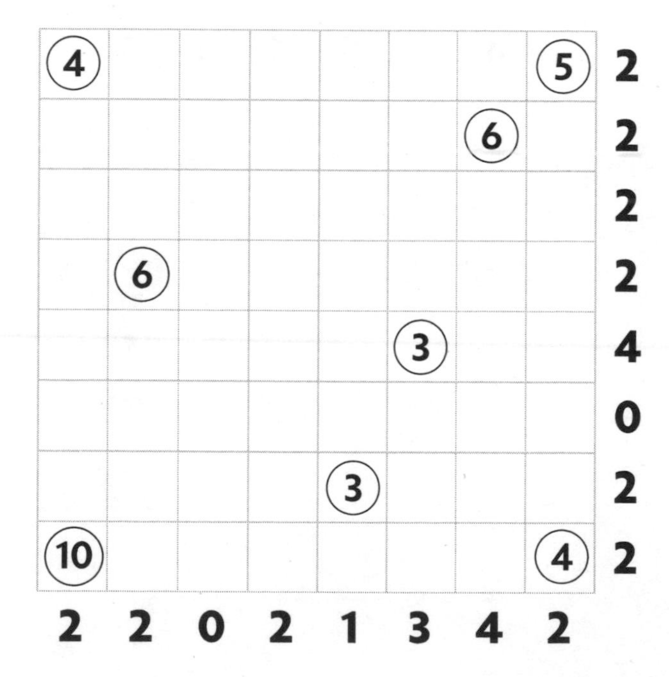

SOLUTION PAGE 175

MEDIUM

						8		1
								1
								0
								2
								0
				6				2
		8						1
7								1
1	1	1	0	1	1	2	1	

SOLUTION PAGE 176

HARD

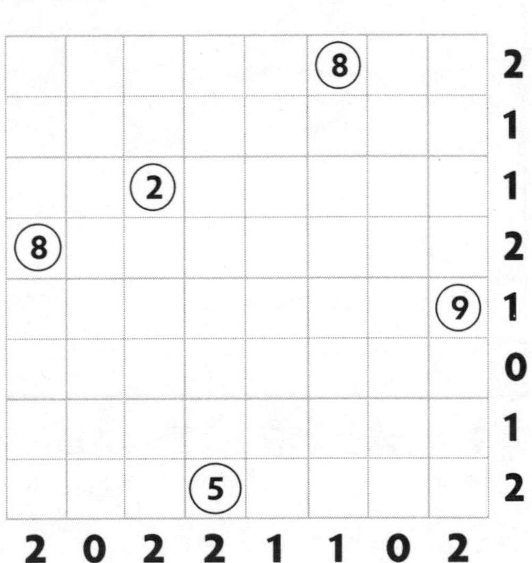

					8			2
								1
		2						1
8								2
							9	1
								0
								1
			5					2
2	0	2	2	1	1	0	2	

SOLUTION PAGE 176

CANDIES

Place numbers from 1 to 6 into the grid so that no number appears more than once in the same row or column. The numbers outside the grid equate to the sum of the numbers in their respective row or column. The numbers in each row must increase from left to right, and in each column must increase from top to bottom.

HARD

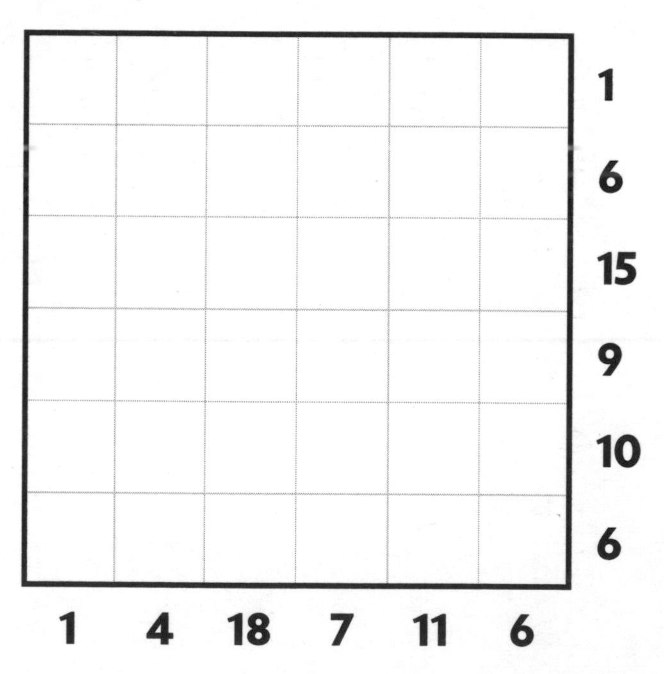

SOLUTION PAGE 176

BAR CODE

Add horizontal and vertical bars – no longer than the length of a single cell – to the grid in such a way that no two bars touch. The numbers outside of the grid equate to the number of bars that appear consecutively in their respective row and column. Where two or more numbers are given, at least one row or column must separate the groups of bars.

HARD

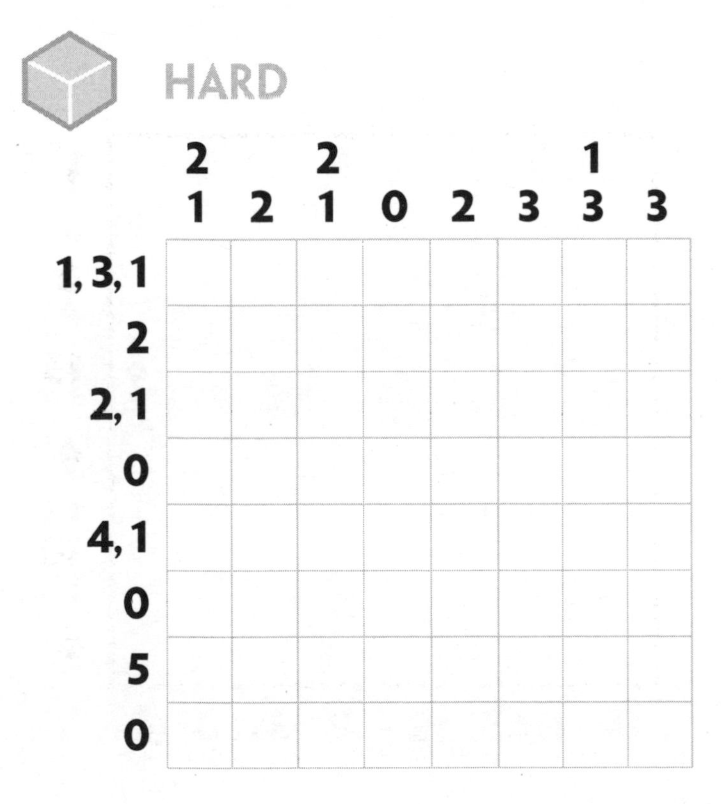

	2 1	2	2 1	0	2	3	1 3	3
1, 3, 1								
2								
2, 1								
0								
4, 1								
0								
5								
0								

SOLUTION PAGE 177

ELBOW ROOM

Draw a horizontal and vertical line from each circled number in an "L" shape. The circled number equates to the number of cells that the lines travel through in total, and the numbers outside of the grid represent the number of lines that finish in each respective row and column. The lines can never intersect.

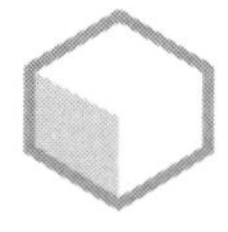

EASY

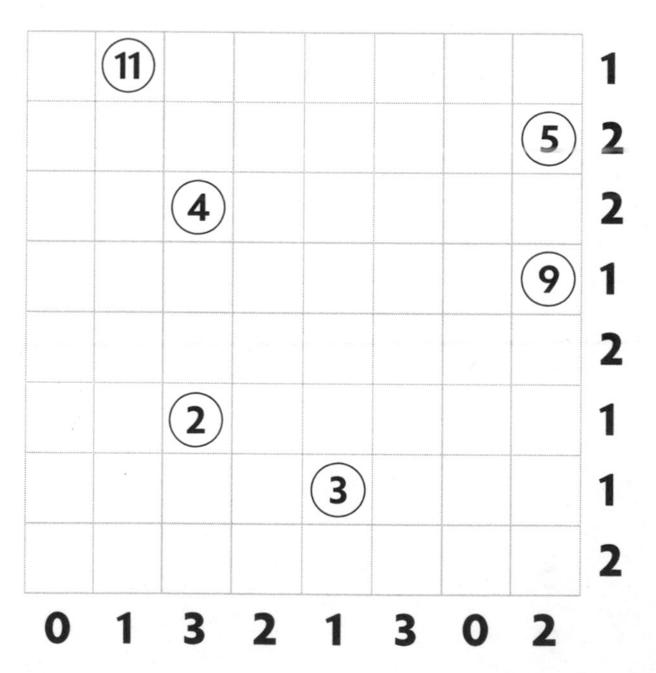

SOLUTION PAGE 177

MEDIUM

						7		1
7								1
		7						1
								0
								1
								2
								1
			7					1
1	0	1	2	1	1	1	1	

SOLUTION PAGE 177

HARD

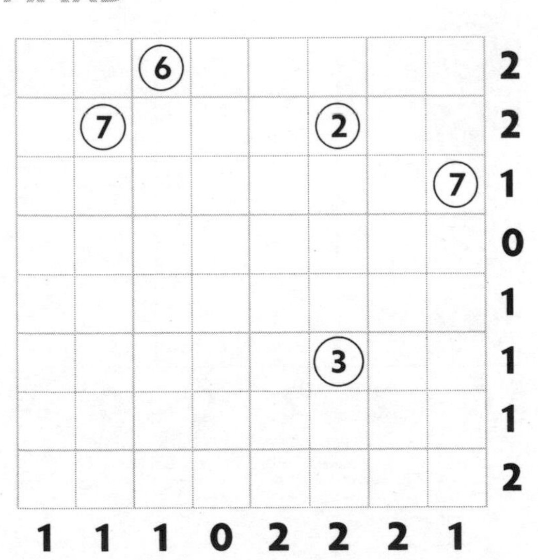

		6						2
	7				2			2
							7	1
								0
								1
					3			1
								1
								2
1	1	1	0	2	2	2	1	

SOLUTION PAGE 178

TARGETS

Place arrows into the cells in the grid to complete the Targets puzzle. The numbers outside of the grid equate to numbers of arrows located in their respective row and column. The arrows can point up, down, left, right or in any diagonal and must be placed so that every target has an arrow heading towards the bullseye. No arrow can shoot through another arrow.

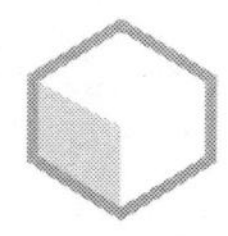

EASY

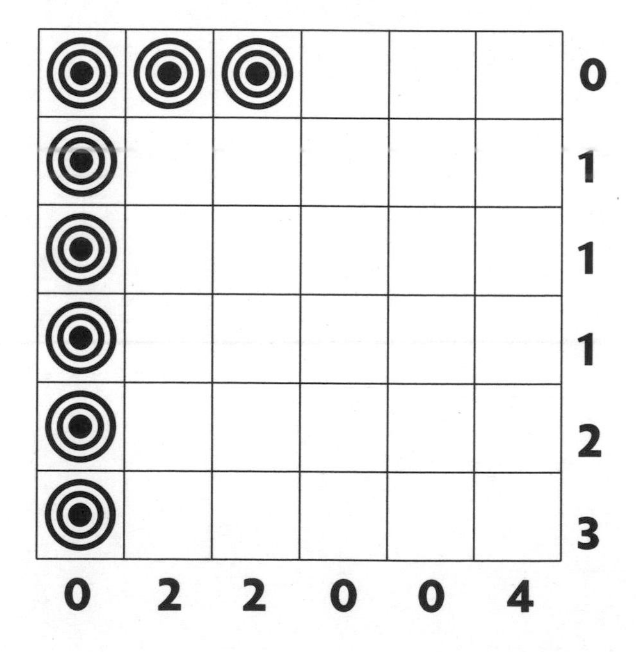

SOLUTION PAGE 178

MEDIUM

						3
		◎				2
		◎	◎			2
	◎	◎				2
	◎	◎	◎			1
		◎	◎	◎		1
3	1	0	1	1	5	

SOLUTION PAGE 178

HARD

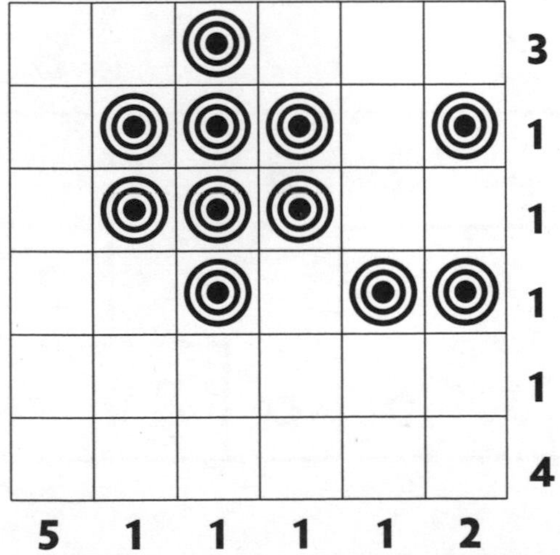

SOLUTION PAGE 179

BOXING MATCH

Place numbers from 1 to 9 into the grid so that the numbers in each bold-lined region are consecutive, and so that every 3x3 grid of squares in the entire puzzle grid sum to the same total.

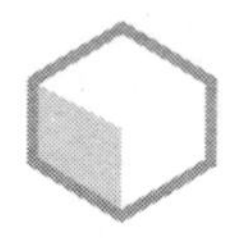

EASY

3		7	4		5
		7	2		
6				8	7
	2	8			
7				2	
	6	6	8		7

SOLUTION PAGE 179

MEDIUM

	7		3		2
	8			6	
6		1		8	
		8			1
	9		3	7	
4		2	5		8

SOLUTION PAGE 179

HARD

	3	2			4
4			7	3	
7		5			
	3				6
	4		5		
3				6	

SOLUTION PAGE 180

CANDIES

Place numbers from 1 to 6 into the grid so that no number appears more than once in the same row or column. The numbers outside the grid equate to the sum of the numbers in their respective row or column. The numbers in each row must increase from left to right, and in each column must increase from top to bottom.

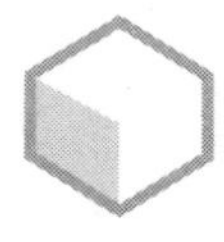

EASY

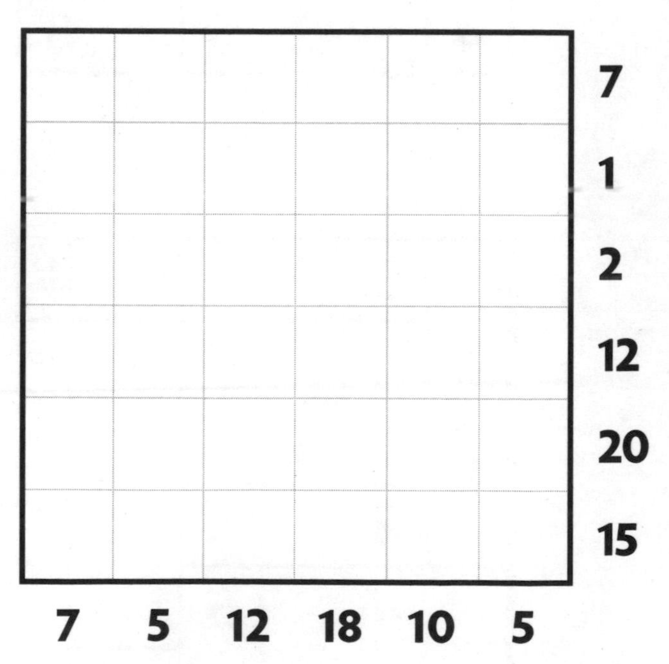

SOLUTION PAGE 180

MEDIUM

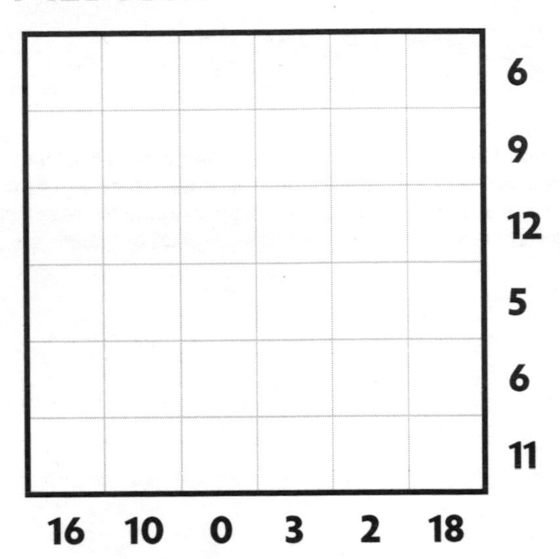

SOLUTION PAGE 180

HARD

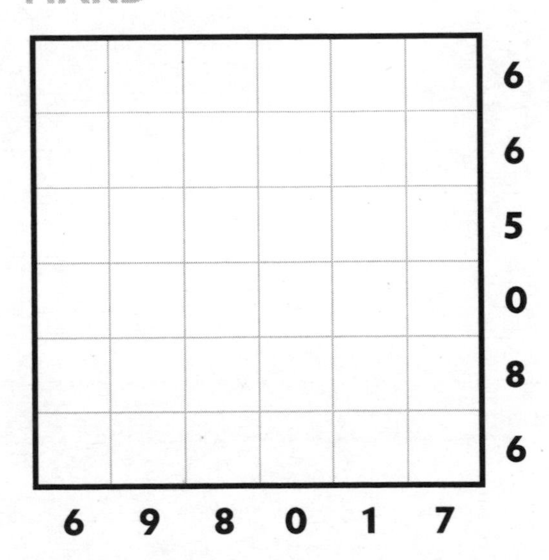

SOLUTION PAGE 181

BAR CODE

Add horizontal and vertical bars – no longer than the length of a single cell – to the grid in such a way that no two bars touch. The numbers outside of the grid equate to the number of bars that appear consecutively in their respective row and column. Where two or more numbers are given, at least one row or column must separate the groups of bars.

HARD

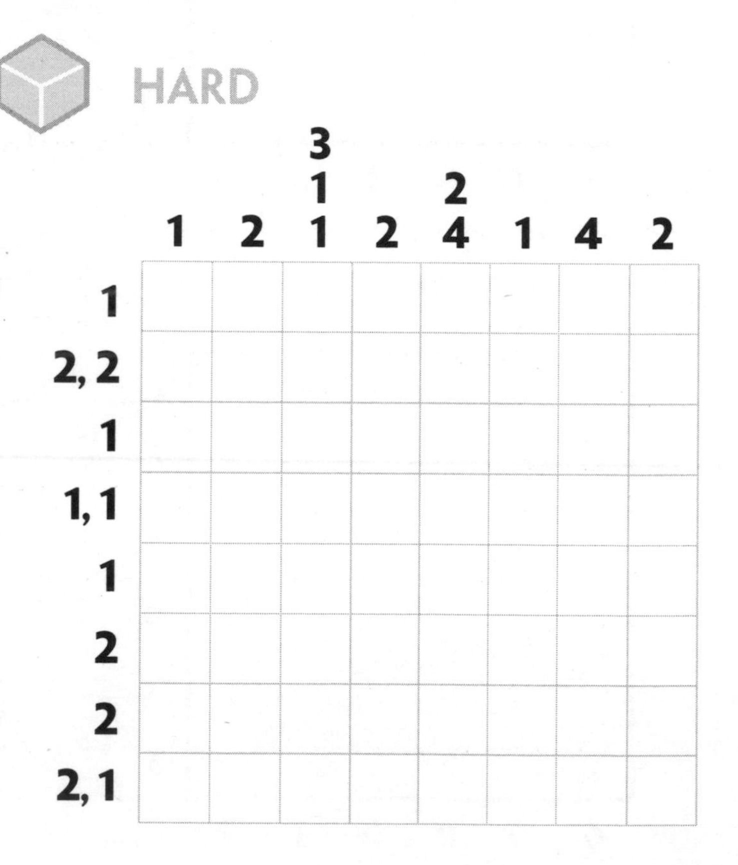

SOLUTION PAGE 181

MATH BOX

Place numbers from 1 to 7 into the grid so that no two numbers appear in the same row or column. Each bold-lined region contains mathematical operations – these must be calculated to solve the puzzle and the questions within – and arrows. The double arrows indicate the direction that the operations must be calculated in, and also represent an equals sign. The single arrows indicate where two digits are joined to create a two-digit number. You may also need to use brackets to complete some of the calculations.

HARD

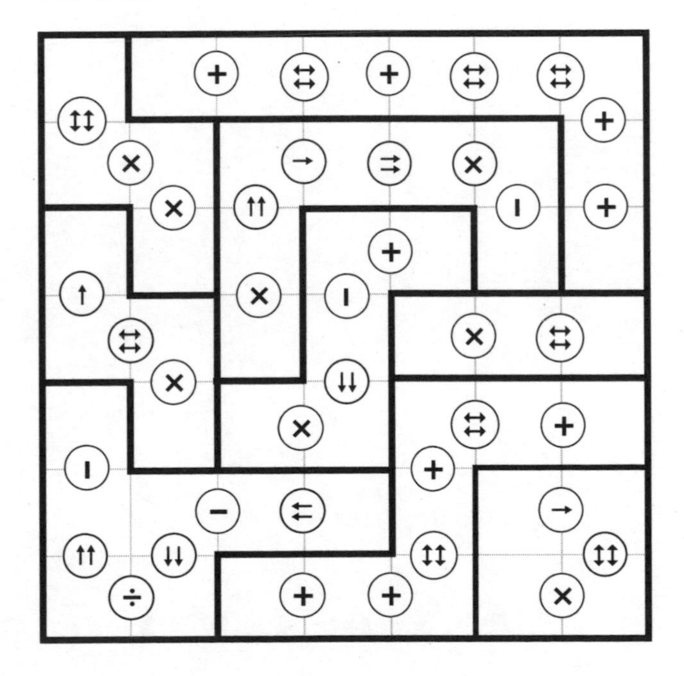

SOLUTION PAGE 181

ELBOW ROOM

Draw a horizontal and vertical line from each circled number in an "L" shape. The circled number equates to the number of cells that the lines travel through in total, and the numbers outside of the grid represent the number of lines that finish in each respective row and column. The lines can never intersect.

HARD

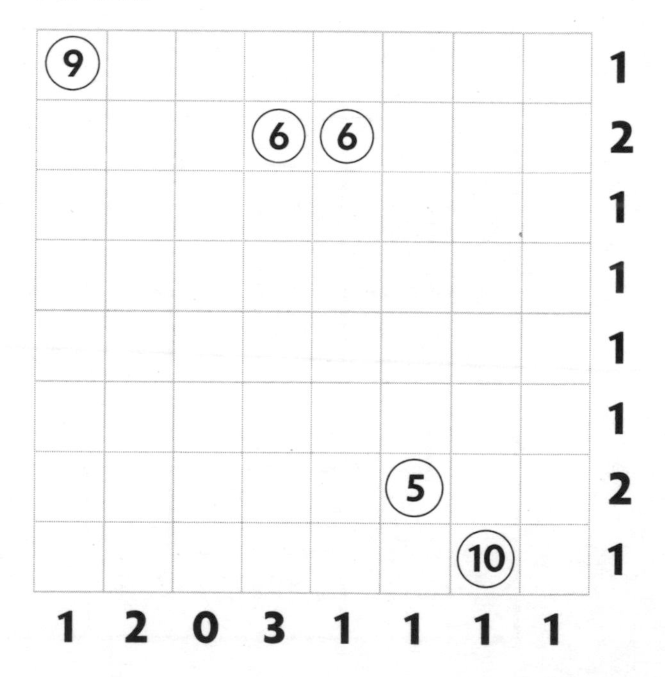

SOLUTION PAGE 182

TARGETS

Place arrows into the cells in the grid to complete the Targets puzzle. The numbers outside of the grid equate to numbers of arrows located in their respective row and column. The arrows can point up, down, left, right or in any diagonal and must be placed so that every target has an arrow heading towards the bullseye. No arrow can shoot through another arrow.

MEDIUM

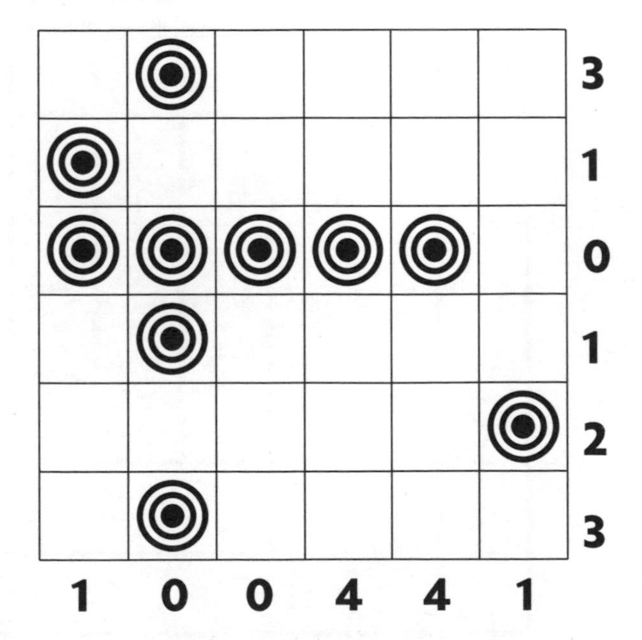

SOLUTION PAGE 182

MATH BOX

Place numbers from 1 to 7 into the grid so that no two numbers appear in the same row or column. Each bold-lined region contains mathematical operations – these must be calculated to solve the puzzle and the questions within – and arrows. The double arrows indicate the direction that the operations must be calculated in, and also represent an equals sign. The single arrows indicate where two digits are joined to create a two-digit number. You may also need to use brackets to complete some of the calculations.

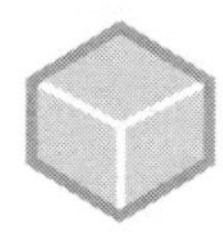

HARD

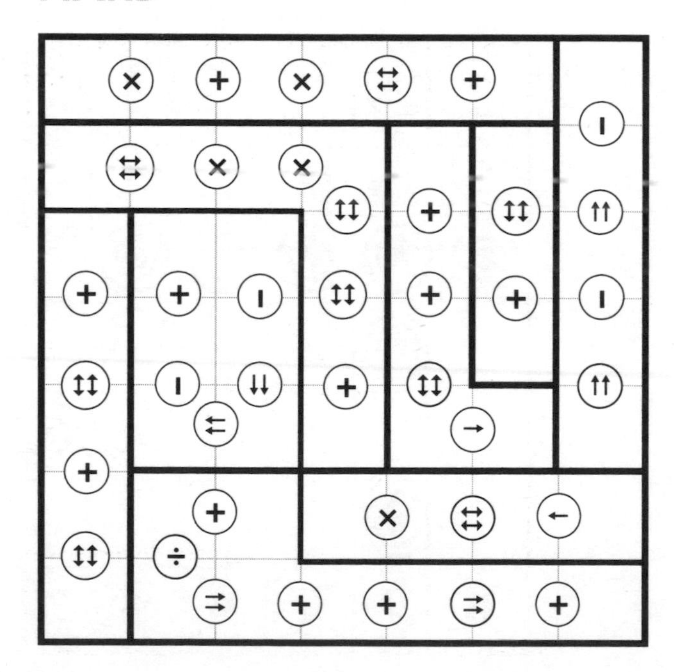

SOLUTION PAGE 182

BOXING MATCH

Place numbers from 1 to 9 into the grid so that the numbers in each bold-lined region are consecutive, and so that every 3x3 grid of squares in the entire puzzle grid sum to the same total.

HARD

3			4	6	
	4				
6		4		5	
		3			5
	3		7		
8			4		4

SOLUTION PAGE 183

BAR CODE

Add horizontal and vertical bars – no longer than the length of a single cell – to the grid in such a way that no two bars touch. The numbers outside of the grid equate to the number of bars that appear consecutively in their respective row and column. Where two or more numbers are given, at least one row or column must separate the groups of bars.

EASY

	1 3	1	2	1	1 1	3
2						
1						
2						
1						
2						
2,1						

SOLUTION PAGE 183

MEDIUM

	1 1	1 1	4	0	0	0	3 3
2							
2							
2							
2							
1, 3							
2							
1, 3							

SOLUTION PAGE 183

HARD

	3	2	1	1 3	1	4	1	4
0								
5								
0								
3								
2								
3, 2								
0								
1, 4								

SOLUTION PAGE 184

ELBOW ROOM

Draw a horizontal and vertical line from each circled number in an "L" shape. The circled number equates to the number of cells that the lines travel through in total, and the numbers outside of the grid represent the number of lines that finish in each respective row and column. The lines can never intersect.

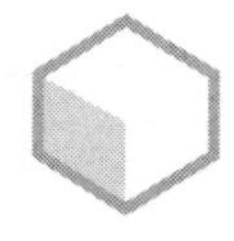

EASY

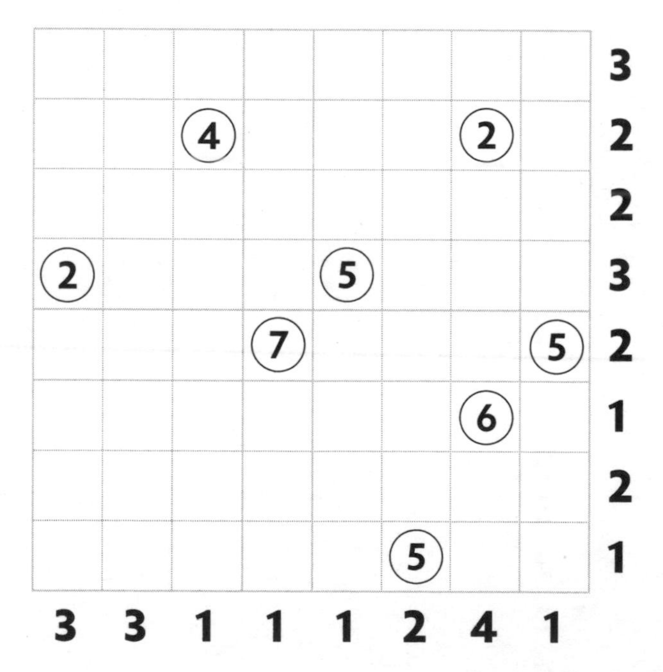

SOLUTION PAGE 184

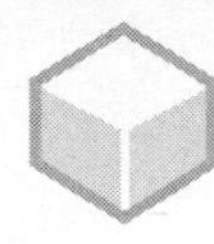

MEDIUM

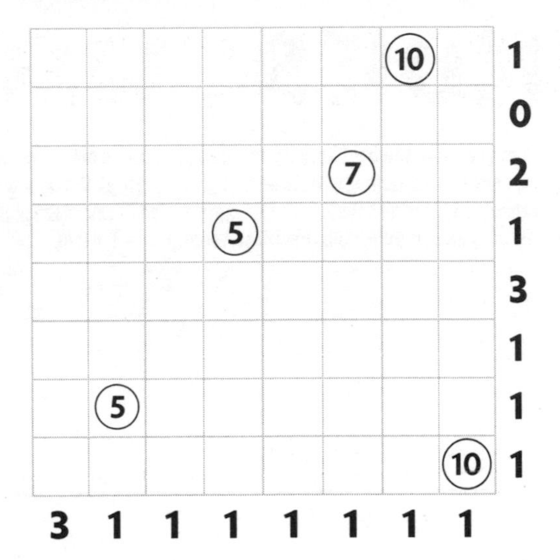

SOLUTION PAGE 184

HARD

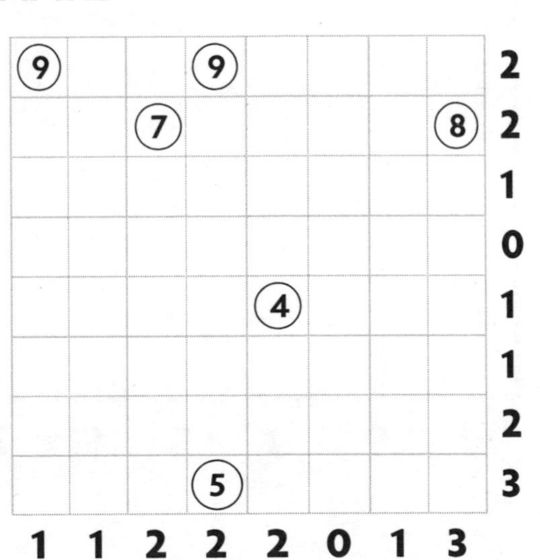

SOLUTION PAGE 185

CANDIES

Place numbers from 1 to 6 into the grid so that no number appears more than once in the same row or column. The numbers outside the grid equate to the sum of the numbers in their respective row or column. The numbers in each row must increase from left to right, and in each column must increase from top to bottom.

HARD

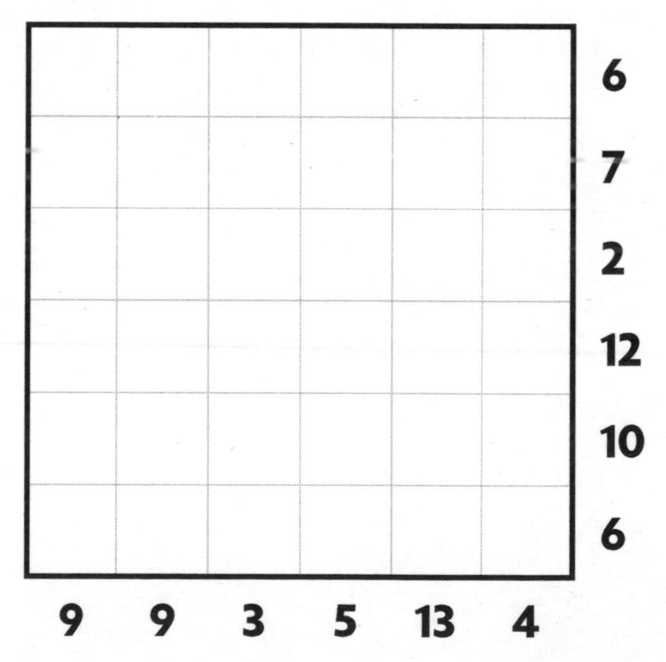

SOLUTION PAGE 185

BAR CODE

Add horizontal and vertical bars – no longer than the length of a single cell – to the grid in such a way that no two bars touch. The numbers outside of the grid equate to the number of bars that appear consecutively in their respective row and column. Where two or more numbers are given, at least one row or column must separate the groups of bars.

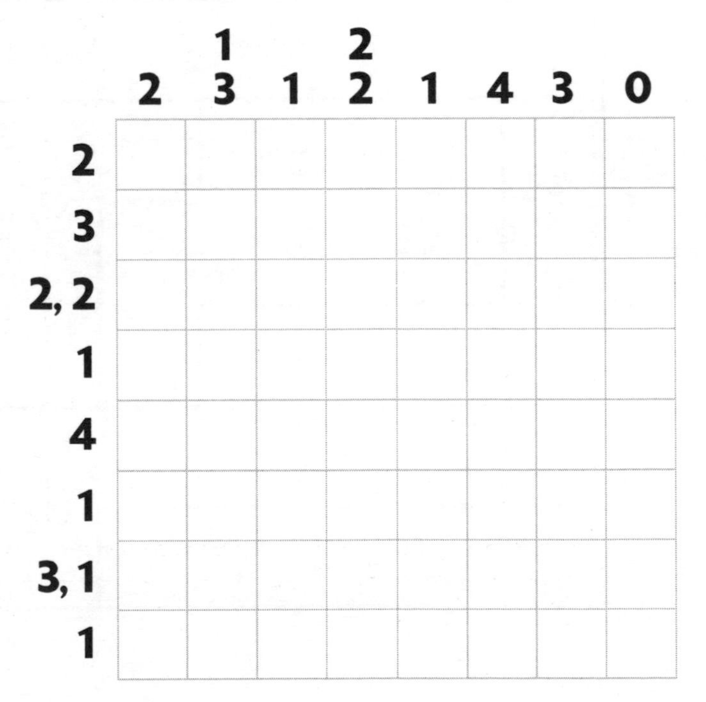

SOLUTION PAGE 185

MATH BOX

Place numbers from 1 to 6 (or 7 in the case of the Hard puzzle) into the grid so that no two numbers appear in the same row or column. Each bold-lined region contains mathematical operations – these must be calculated to solve the puzzle and the questions within – and arrows. The double arrows indicate the direction that the operations must be calculated in, and also represent an equals sign. The single arrows indicate where two digits are joined to create a two-digit number. You may also need to use brackets to complete some of the calculations.

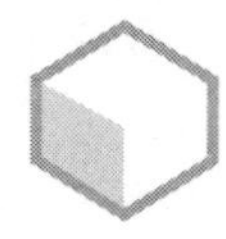

EASY

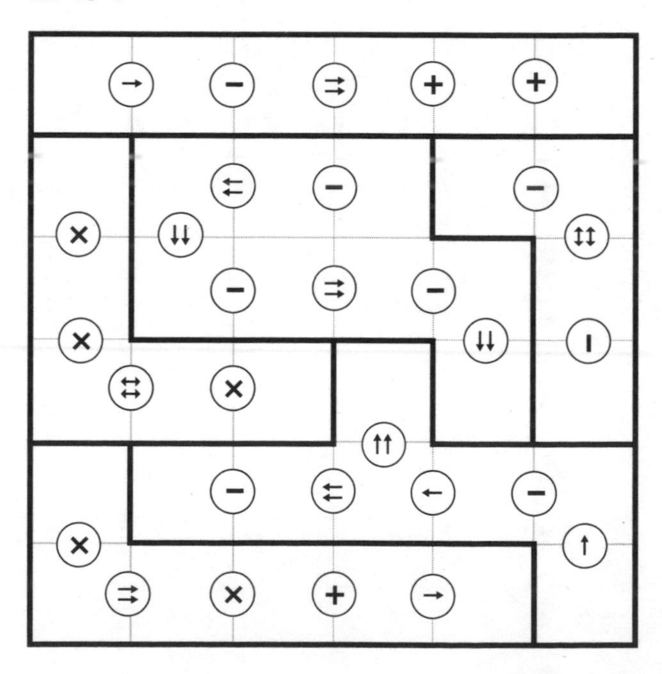

SOLUTION PAGE 186

MEDIUM

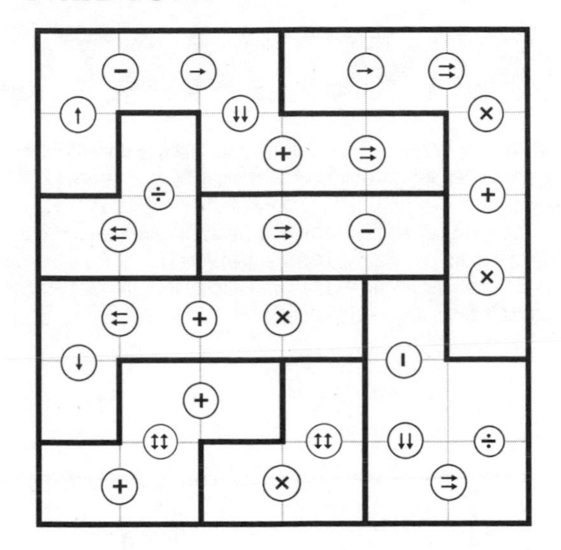

SOLUTION PAGE 186

HARD

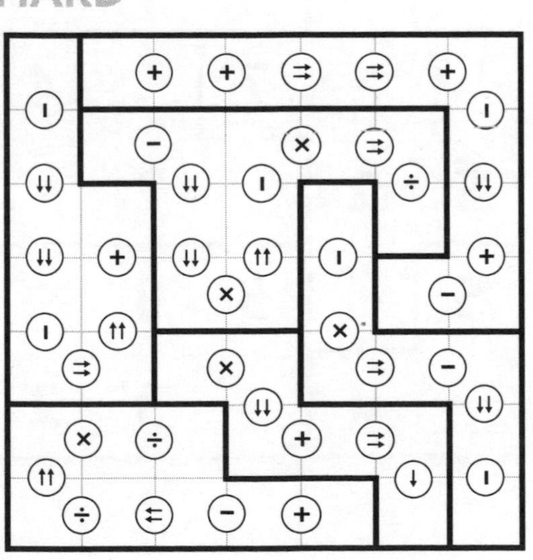

SOLUTION PAGE 186

BOXING MATCH

Place numbers from 1 to 9 into the grid so that the numbers in each bold-lined region are consecutive, and so that every 3x3 grid of squares in the entire puzzle grid sum to the same total.

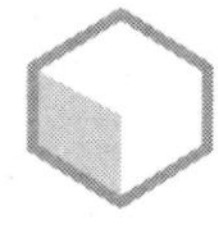

EASY

4			1		4
	4		8		
		7		4	
5	2		2		7
5		5	8		6
	4		3	2	

SOLUTION PAGE 187

MEDIUM

	3			3	
4					5
5		2			
	2		6	2	
			2		5
4		3			2

SOLUTION PAGE 187

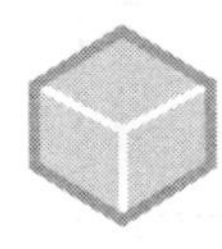

HARD

4			2		5
		3			4
8					
	5			3	
		6		3	
7			8		8

SOLUTION PAGE 187

ELBOW ROOM

Draw a horizontal and vertical line from each circled number in an "L" shape. The circled number equates to the number of cells that the lines travel through in total, and the numbers outside of the grid represent the number of lines that finish in each respective row and column. The lines can never intersect.

HARD

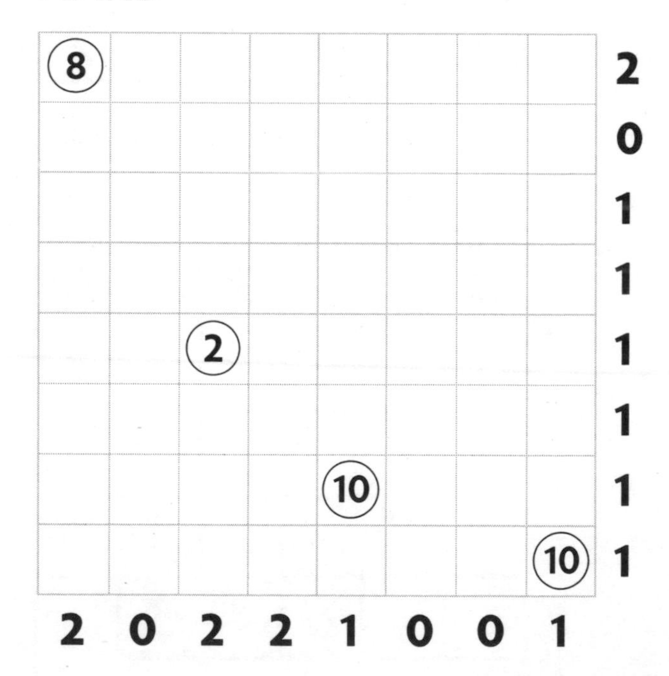

SOLUTION PAGE 188

BAR CODE

Add horizontal and vertical bars – no longer than the length of a single cell – to the grid in such a way that no two bars touch. The numbers outside of the grid equate to the number of bars that appear consecutively in their respective row and column. Where two or more numbers are given, at least one row or column must separate the groups of bars.

HARD

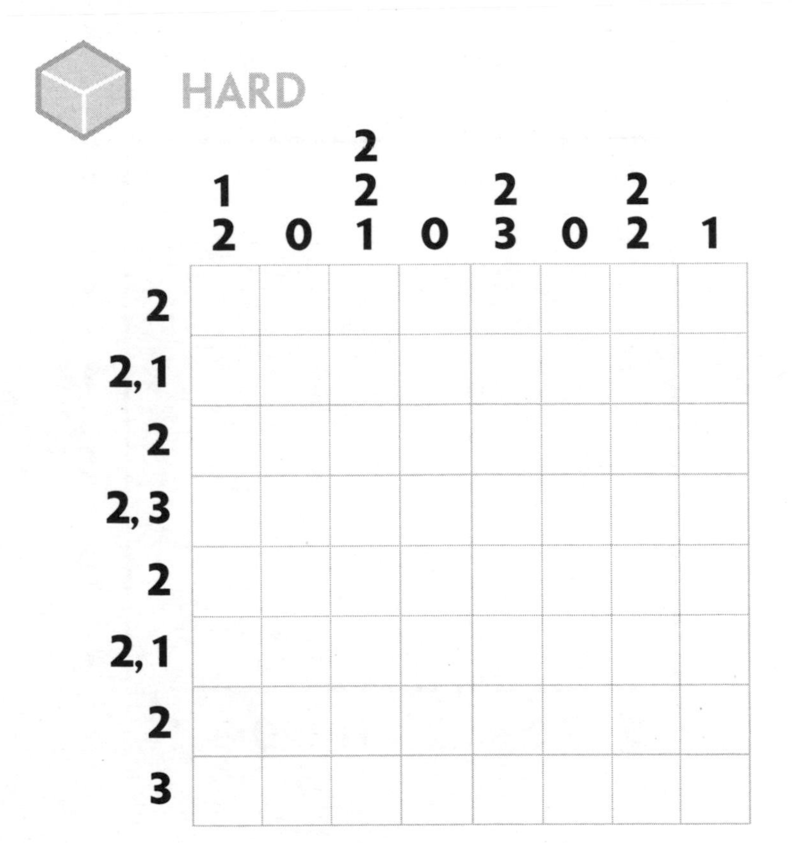

SOLUTION PAGE 188

CANDIES

Place numbers from 1 to 6 into the grid so that no number appears more than once in the same row or column. The numbers outside the grid equate to the sum of the numbers in their respective row or column. The numbers in each row must increase from left to right, and in each column must increase from top to bottom.

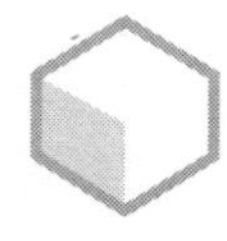

EASY

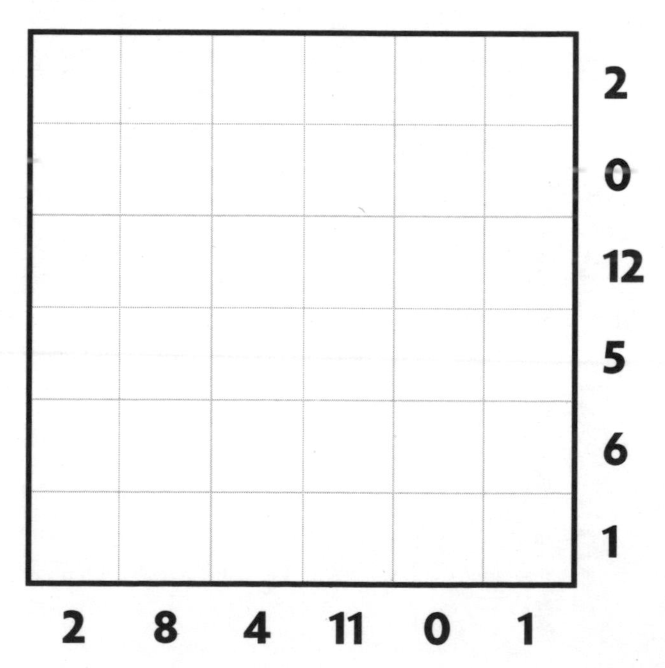

SOLUTION PAGE 188

MEDIUM

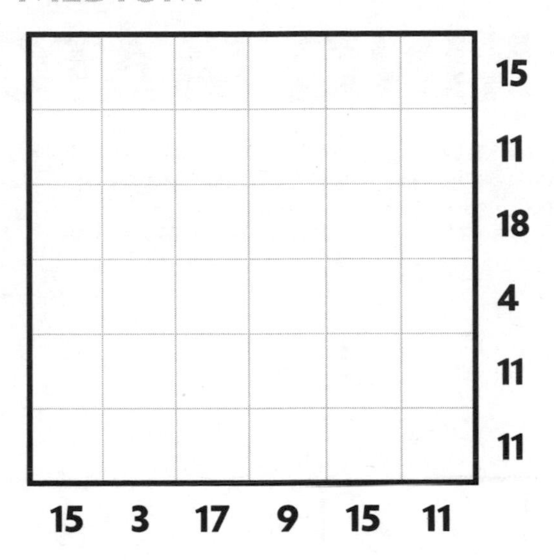

SOLUTION PAGE 189

HARD

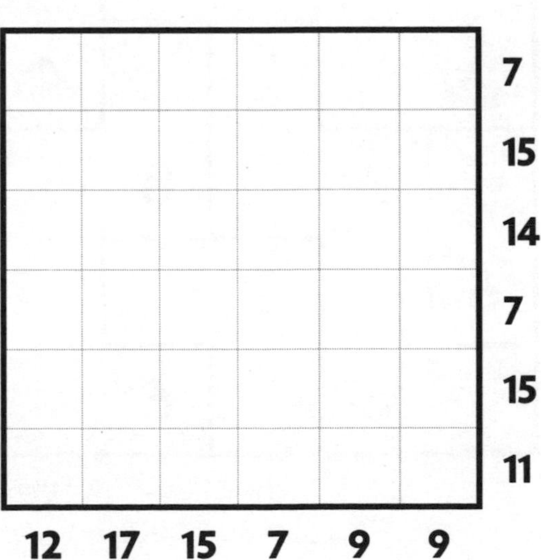

SOLUTION PAGE 189

BOXING MATCH

Place numbers from 1 to 9 into the grid so that the numbers in each bold-lined region are consecutive, and so that every 3x3 grid of squares in the entire puzzle grid sum to the same total.

HARD

	6	5		8	
4		2			
				4	
	7		8		4
6		2			
	6		6		3

SOLUTION PAGE 189

MATH BOX

Place numbers from 1 to 7 into the grid so that no two numbers appear in the same row or column. Each bold-lined region contains mathematical operations – these must be calculated to solve the puzzle and the questions within – and arrows. The double arrows indicate the direction that the operations must be calculated in, and also represent an equals sign. The single arrows indicate where two digits are joined to create a two-digit number. You may also need to use brackets to complete some of the calculations.

HARD

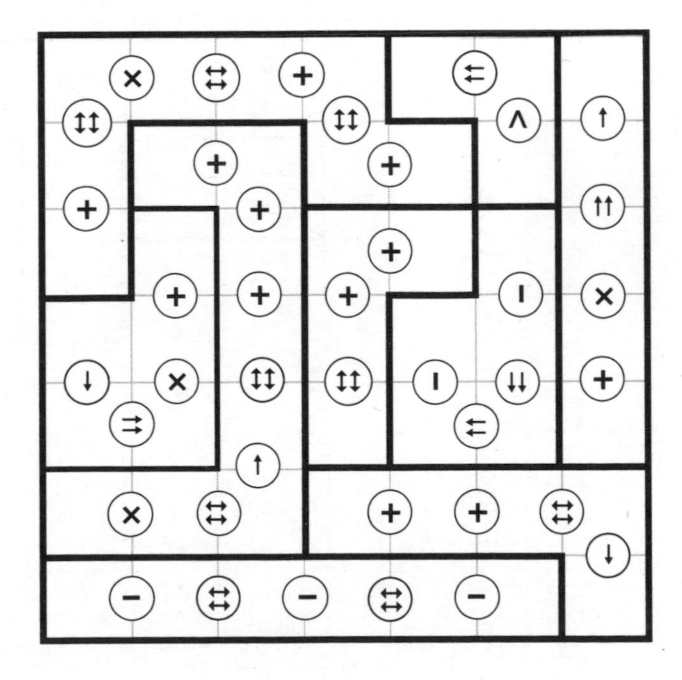

SOLUTION PAGE 189

SOLUTIONS

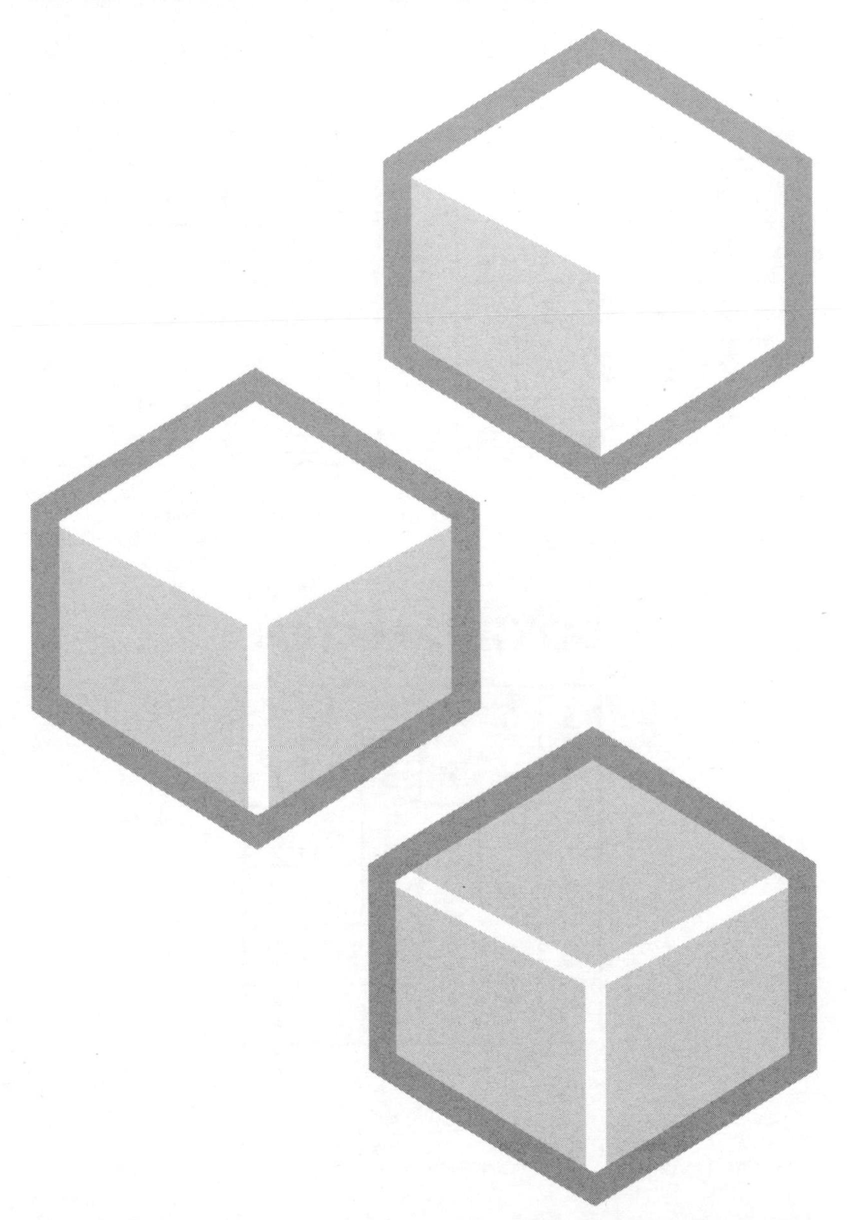

BOXING MATCH

3	2	3	4	1	5
7	5	6	5	2	6
4	3	8	5	7	6
1	2	5	2	1	7
5	7	6	3	4	6
4	3	8	5	7	6

EASY

BOXING MATCH

3	4	8	4	6	5
5	7	3	5	3	4
6	2	4	5	4	6
1	6	8	2	8	5
7	6	2	7	2	3
3	4	5	2	6	7

MEDIUM

BOXING MATCH

3	5	4	6	4	3
4	7	8	5	7	5
7	5	4	3	6	8
2	6	4	5	5	3
8	6	5	9	6	2
6	7	3	2	8	7

HARD

CANDIES

	1	2	3	4		10
	2	3			4	9
			4	5	6	15
1	3	4	5	6		19
2	4	5	6			17
3	5	6				14
6	15	20	18	15	10	

EASY

BAR CODE

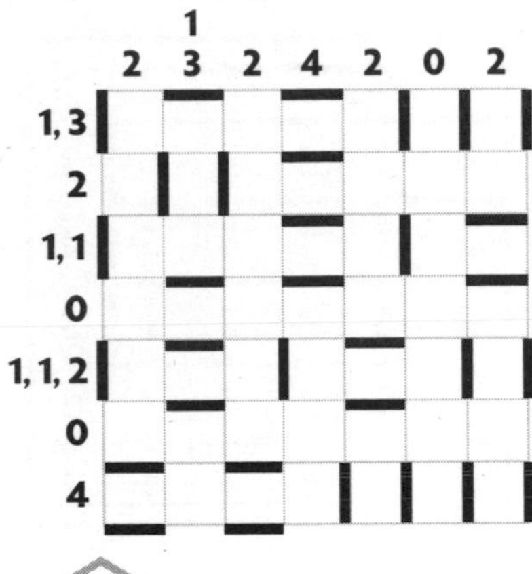

MEDIUM

MATH BOX

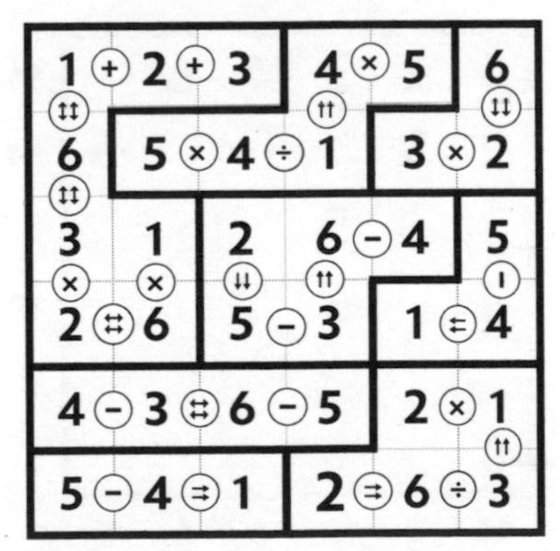

EASY

MATH BOX

6	4	3	5	2	1
4	2	5	1	6	3
2	3	1	6	5	4
3	6	4	2	1	5
1	5	2	4	3	6
5	1	6	3	4	2

MEDIUM

MATH BOX

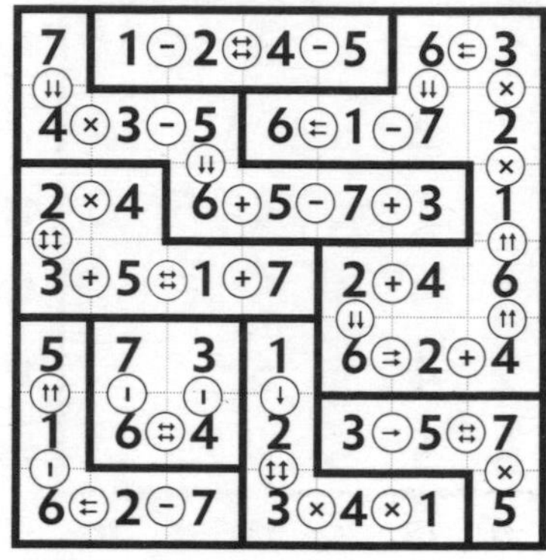

HARD

CANDIES

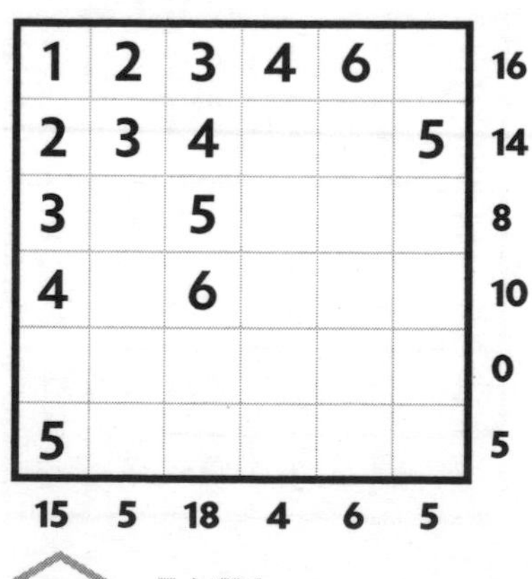

EASY

CANDIES

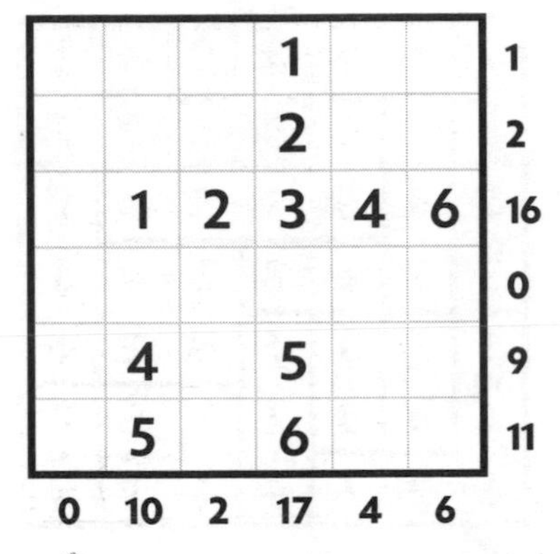

MEDIUM

CANDIES

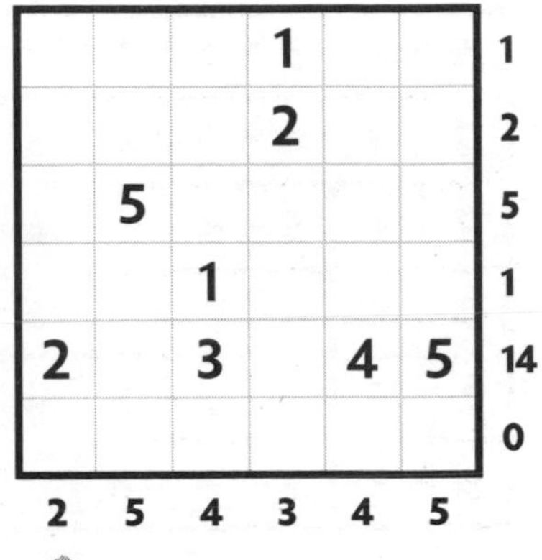

HARD

MATH BOX

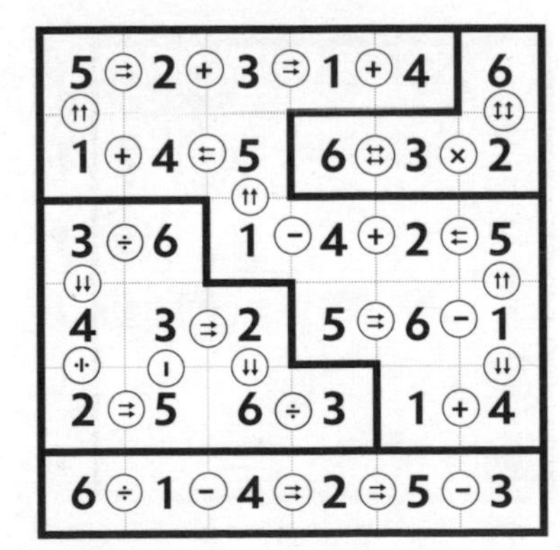

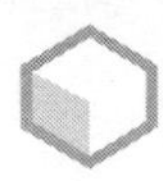
EASY

MATH BOX

5	4	3	6	1	2
2	1	6	5	4	3
1	2	5	4	3	6
3	6	4	1	2	5
6	3	1	2	5	4
4	5	2	3	6	1

MEDIUM

MATH BOX

7	6	4	2	3	1	5
3	5	1	4	6	7	2
5	4	3	1	2	6	7
2	7	6	3	5	4	1
1	3	7	5	4	2	6
4	1	2	6	7	5	3
6	2	5	7	1	3	4

HARD

TARGETS

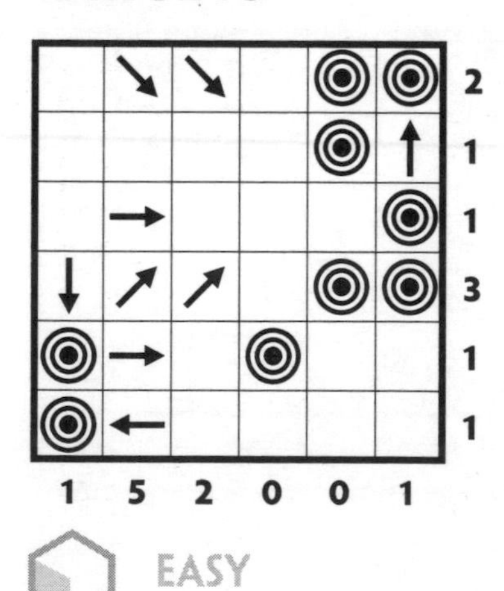

EASY

TARGETS

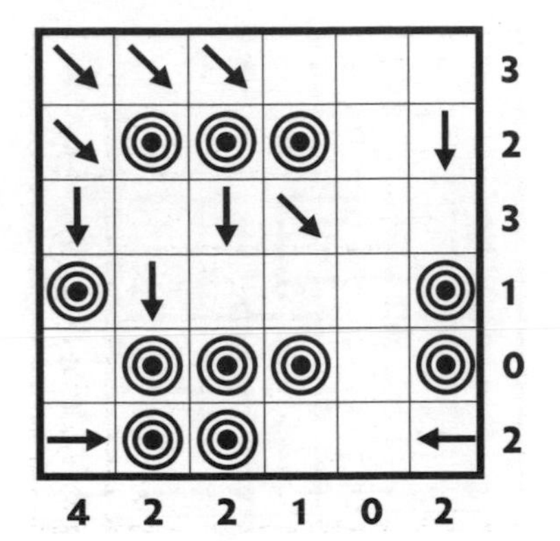

MEDIUM

TARGETS

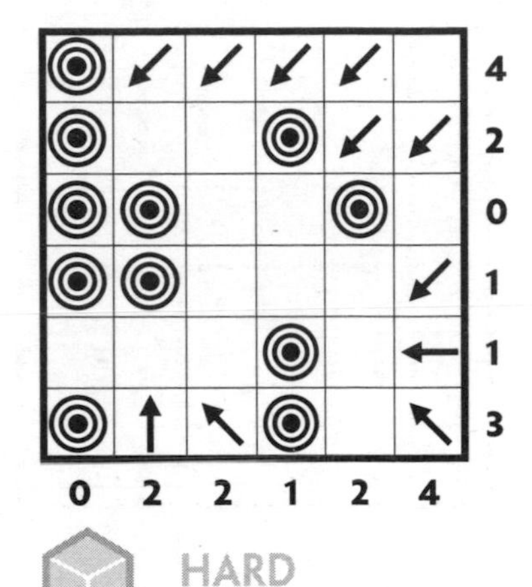

HARD

BOXING MATCH

3	5	4	1	2	5
2	3	4	5	4	3
5	1	6	4	3	6
6	4	2	4	1	3
1	5	3	4	6	2
2	3	7	1	5	7

EASY

BAR CODE

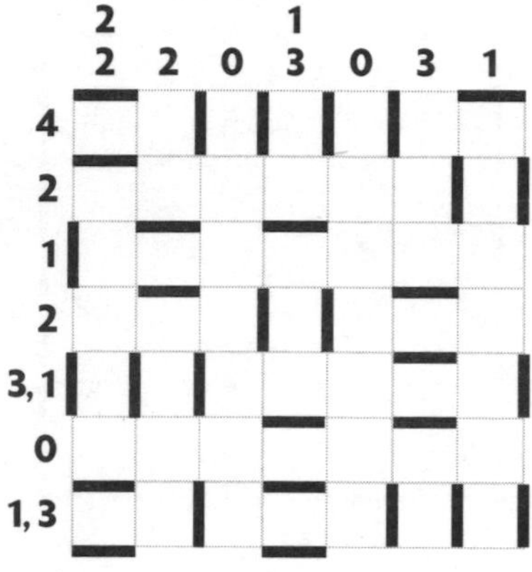

BOXING MATCH

4	6	3	5	4	4
7	2	4	5	6	5
6	3	5	7	1	3
7	5	1	8	3	2
5	2	6	3	6	7
4	6	4	5	4	2

EASY

BOXING MATCH

1	2	3	2	3	6
5	6	5	4	5	2
3	4	7	3	4	7
3	2	1	4	3	4
4	5	7	3	4	4
6	3	5	6	3	5

MEDIUM

BOXING MATCH

1	2	5	6	5	7
8	4	6	6	5	8
9	7	5	6	3	1
1	4	3	6	7	5
9	7	2	7	8	4
8	7	6	5	3	2

HARD

ELBOW ROOM

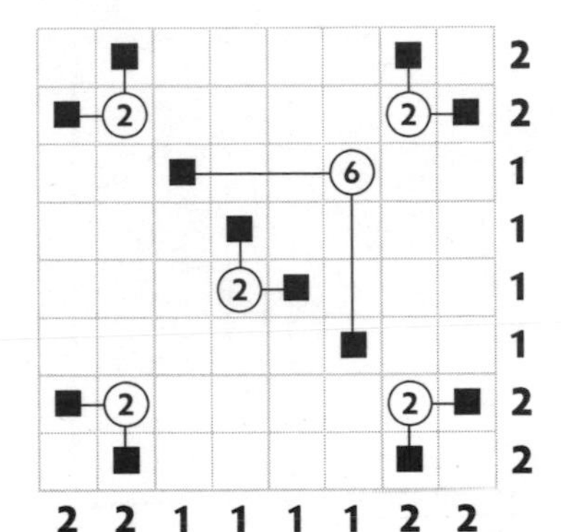

EASY

BAR CODE

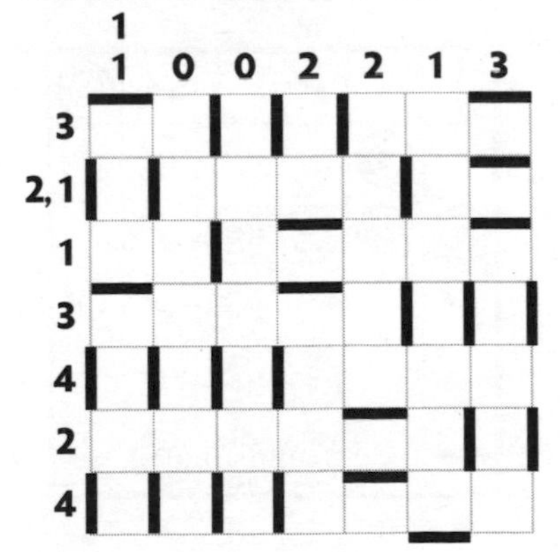

MEDIUM

CANDIES

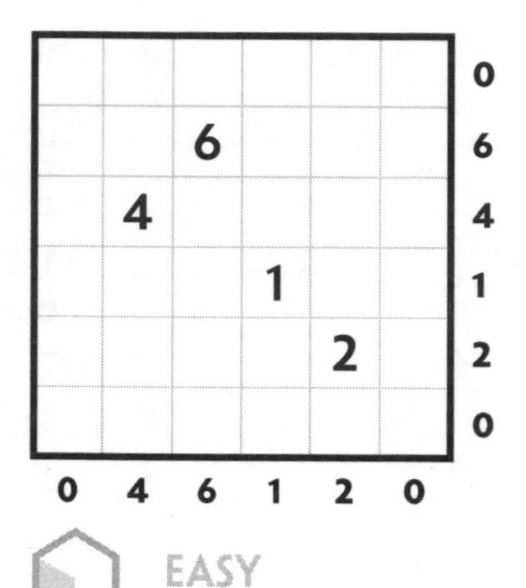

EASY

MATH BOX

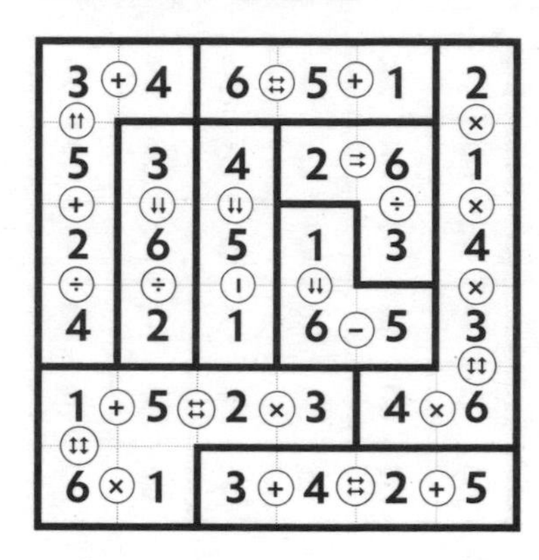

EASY

TARGETS

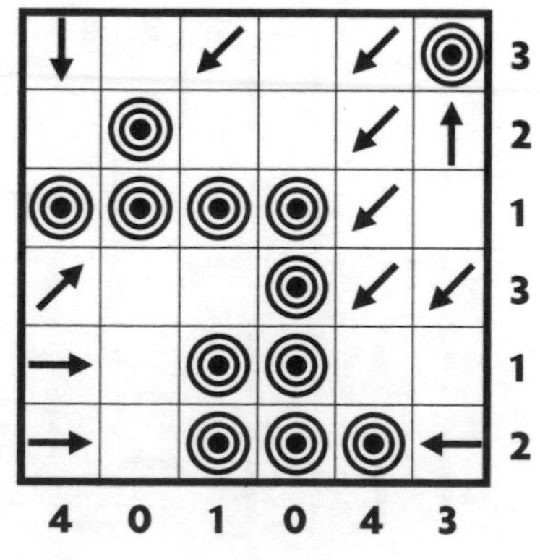

MEDIUM

BOXING MATCH

3	4	4	3	2	2
2	6	5	3	8	7
5	7	6	4	7	6
1	4	6	1	2	4
3	5	5	4	7	7
7	8	3	6	8	3

ELBOW ROOM

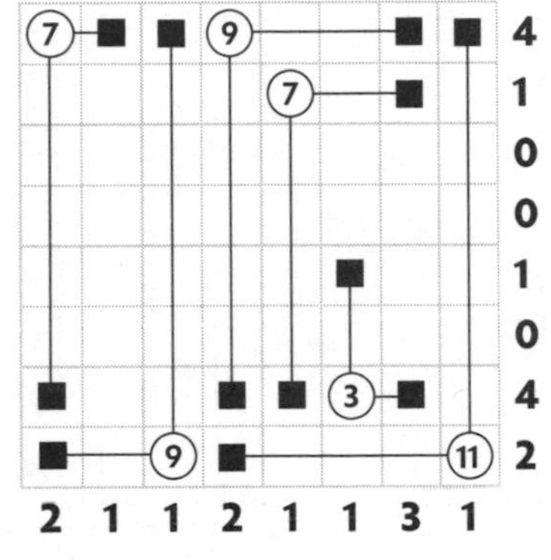

ELBOW ROOM

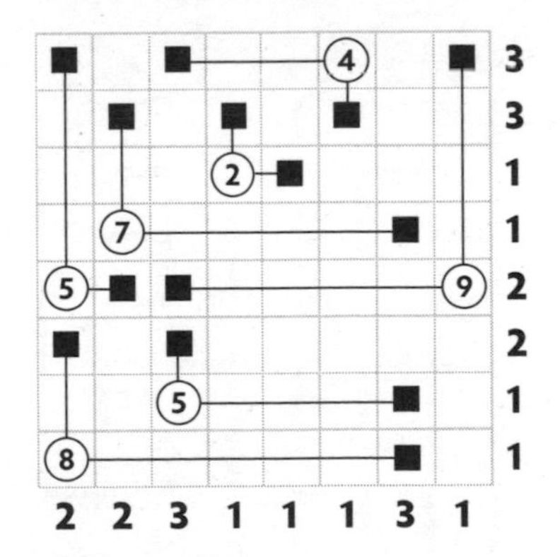

ELBOW ROOM

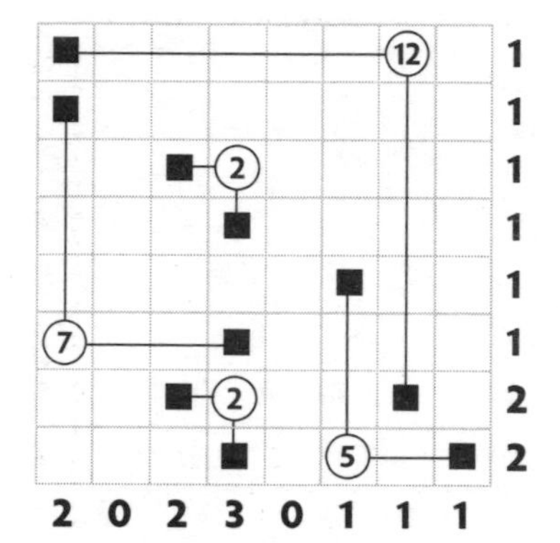

HARD

ELBOW ROOM

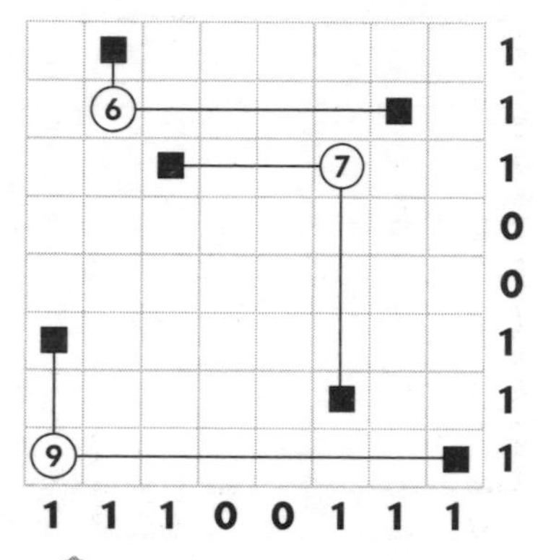

MEDIUM

BAR CODE

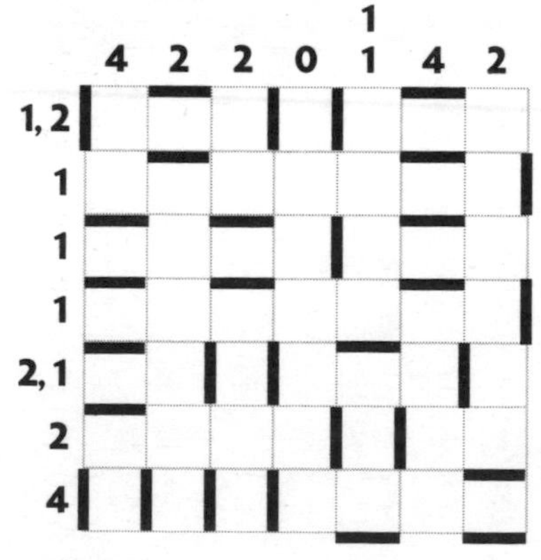

MEDIUM

CANDIES

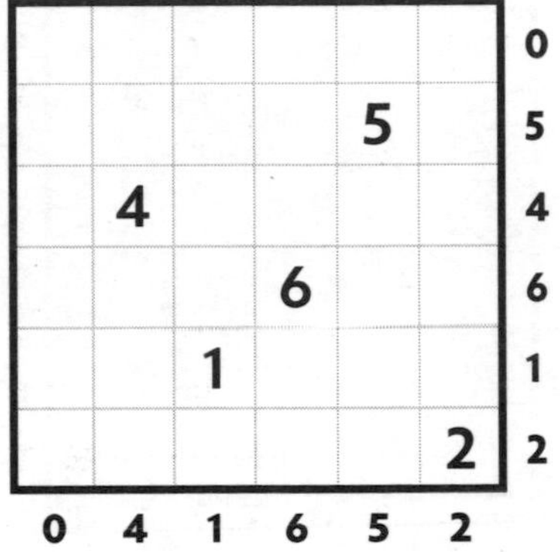

						0
				5		5
	4					4
			6			6
		1				1
					2	2
0	4	1	6	5	2	

EASY

CANDIES

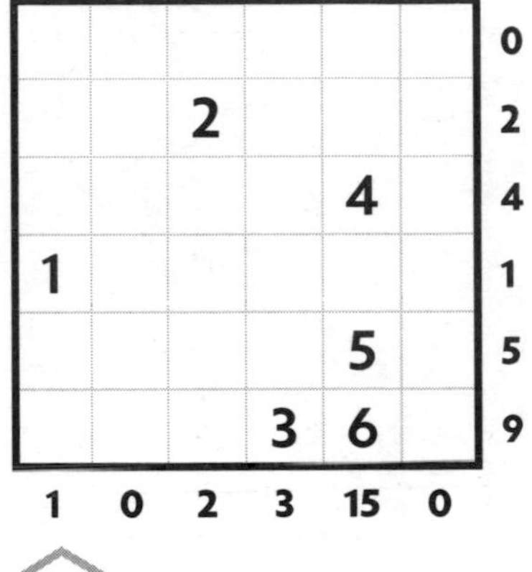

						0
		2				2
				4		4
1						1
				5		5
			3	6		9
1	0	2	3	15	0	

MEDIUM

CANDIES

1	2	3	4	5		15
2	3	4	5			14
3	4	5				12
4	5					9
5						5
					6	6
15	14	12	9	5	6	

HARD

TARGETS

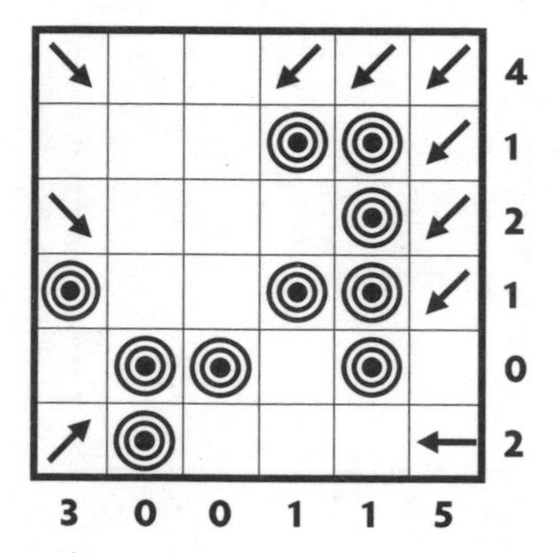

EASY

TARGETS

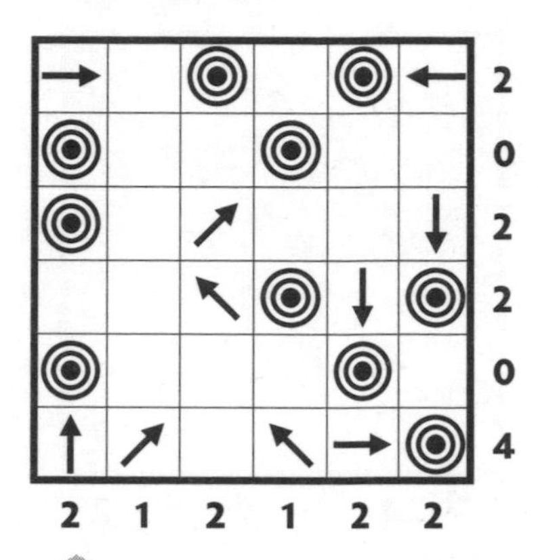

MEDIUM

TARGETS

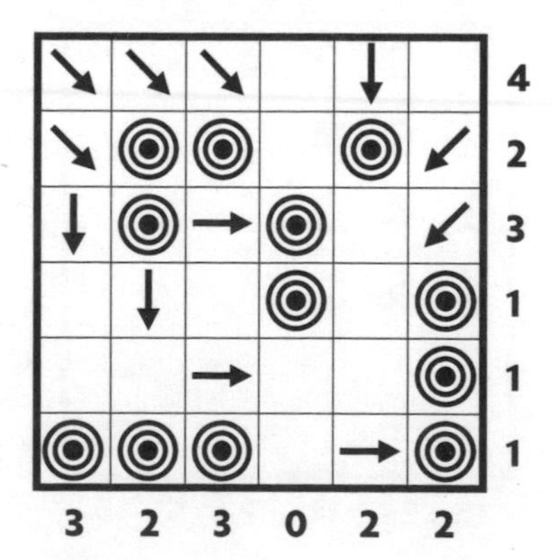

HARD

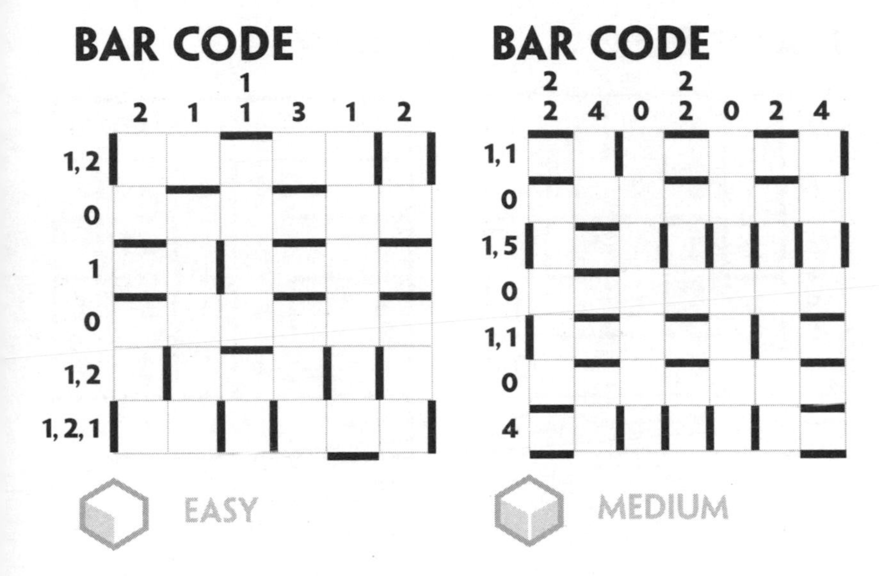
BAR CODE
1
2 1 1 3 1 2
1, 2
0
1
0
1, 2
1, 2, 1
EASY
BAR CODE
2 2
2 4 0 2 0 2 4
1, 1
0
1, 5
0
1, 1
0
4
MEDIUM

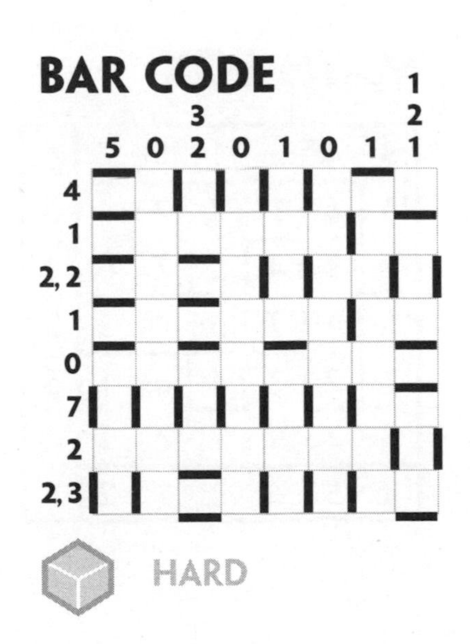
BAR CODE
1
3 2
5 0 2 0 1 0 1 1
4
1
2, 2
1
0
7
2
2, 3
HARD

MATH BOX

2	6	1	4	3	5
6	3	5	2	1	4
4	2	3	1	5	6
3	4	2	5	6	1
1	5	6	3	4	2
5	1	4	6	2	3

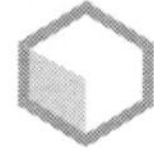

EASY

MATH BOX

5	4	6	3	1	2
1	6	5	2	3	4
3	5	2	6	4	1
6	2	4	1	5	3
4	1	3	5	2	6
2	3	1	4	6	5

MEDIUM

MATH BOX

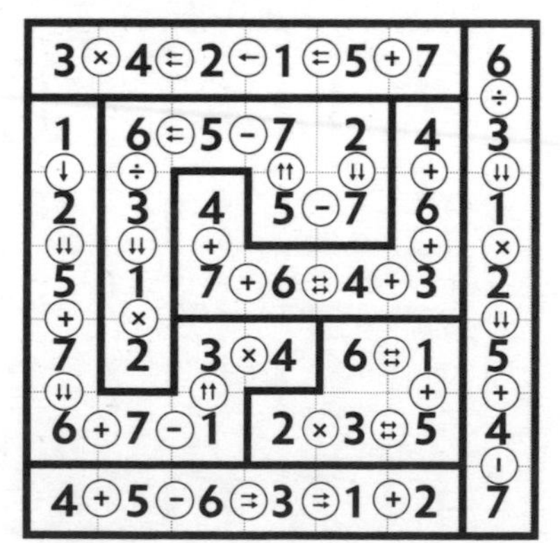

HARD

BAR CODE

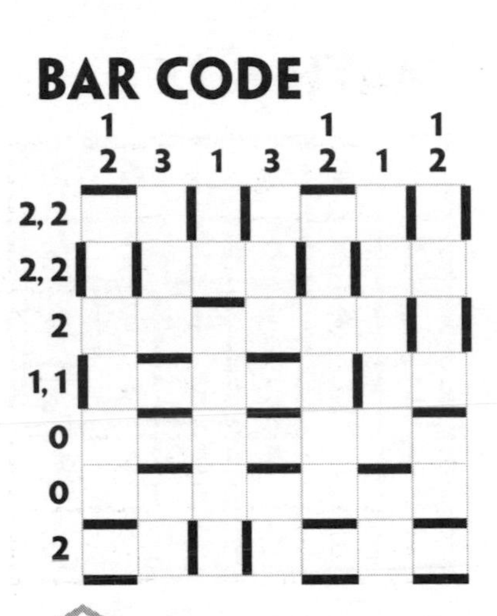

MEDIUM

MATH BOX

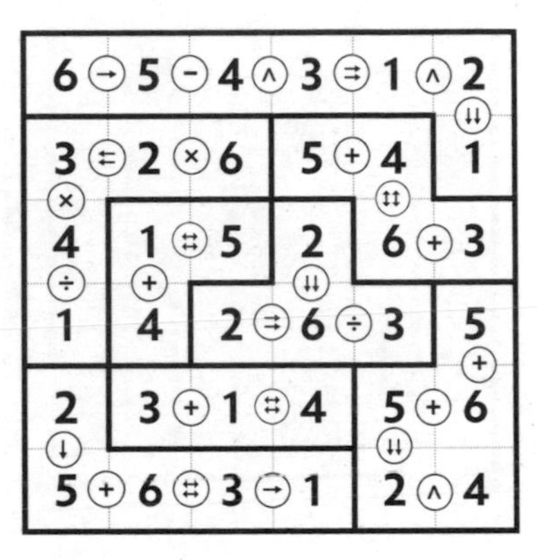

MEDIUM

CANDIES

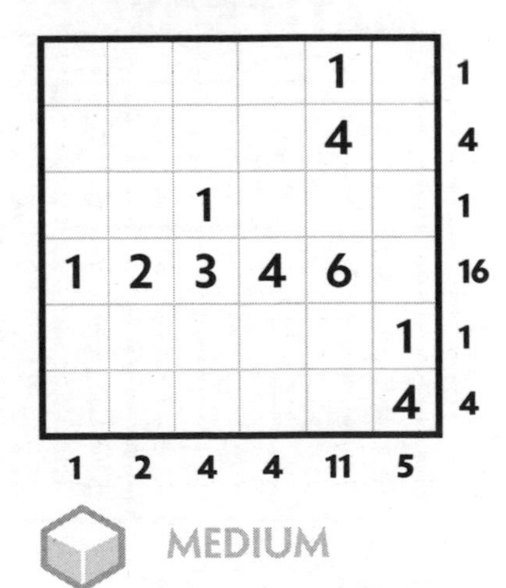

MEDIUM

TARGETS

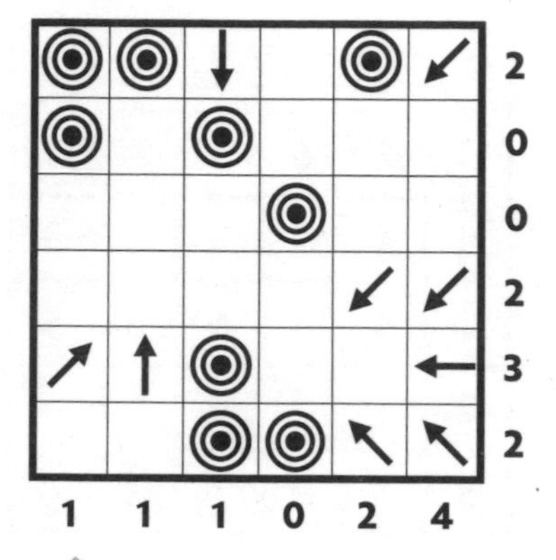

MEDIUM

MATH BOX

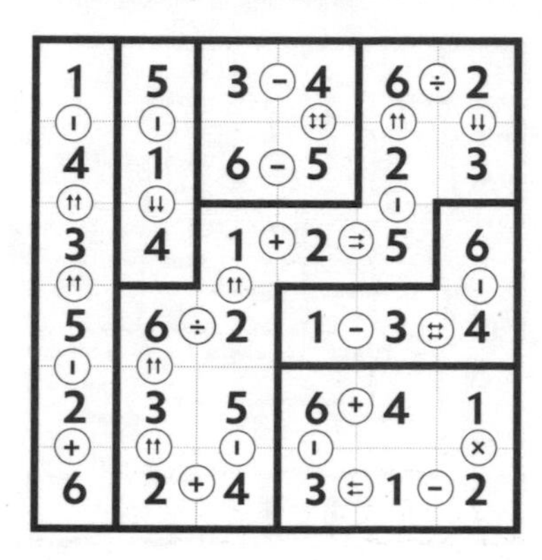

EASY

MATH BOX

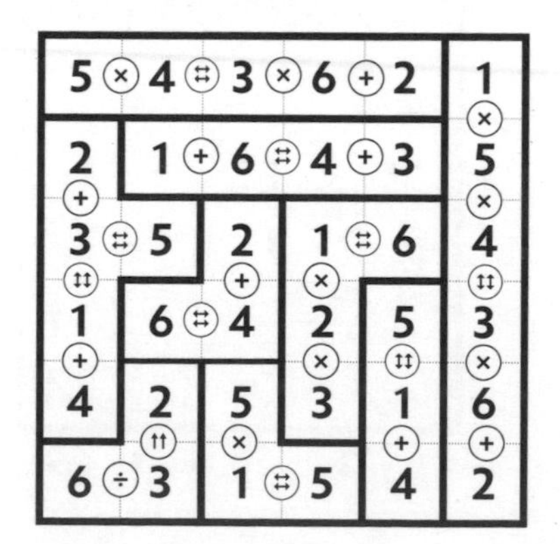

MEDIUM

MATH BOX

6		1	→	2		3		5	+	7	−	4
÷		↑↑				÷		+				↓↓
3		5		4	⇄	6		7		2		1
×		+		−						+		↓
1		7		6		2	×	3	⇄	4		5
×												↓↓
4		6		3		7	+	1	+	5	+	2
↑↑		⇅		↓↓								
5		2		7	−	4		6	←	1	⇄	3
−		+										+
7		4	⇄	1	+	5	⇄	2	×	3		6
↑↑												+
2	⇆	3	−	5	⇆	1	×	4	−	6		7

HARD

ELBOW ROOM

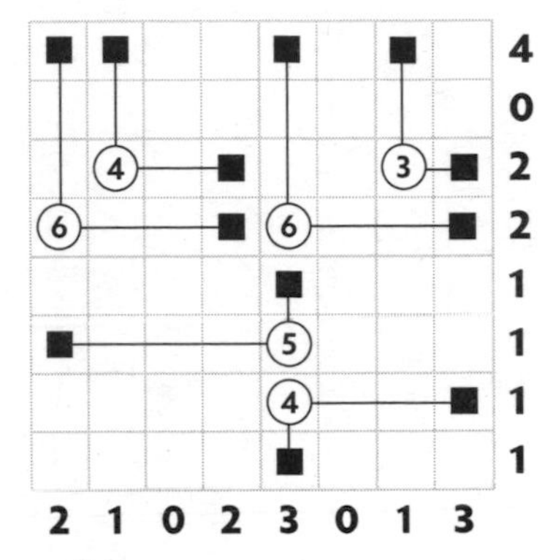

EASY

ELBOW ROOM

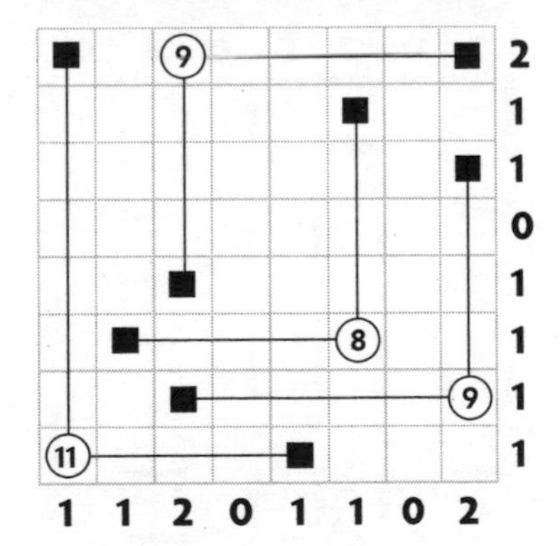

MEDIUM

ELBOW ROOM

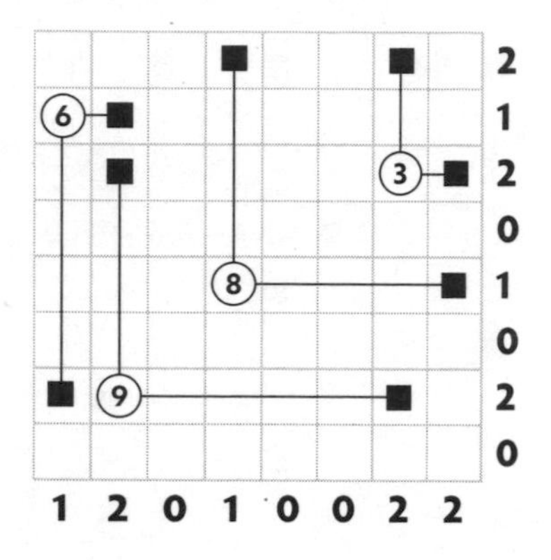

HARD

BAR CODE

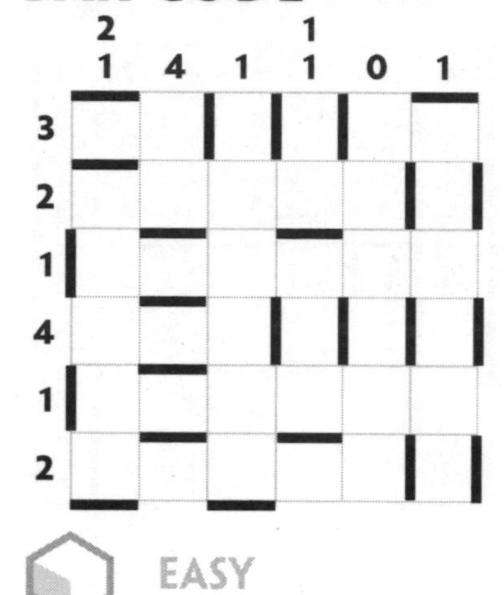

EASY

BAR CODE

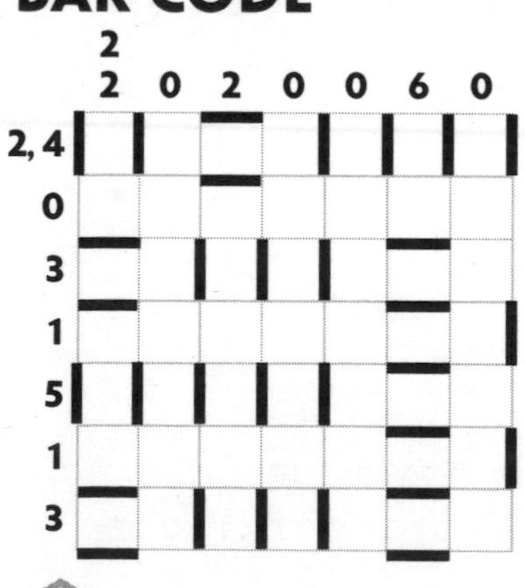

MEDIUM

BAR CODE

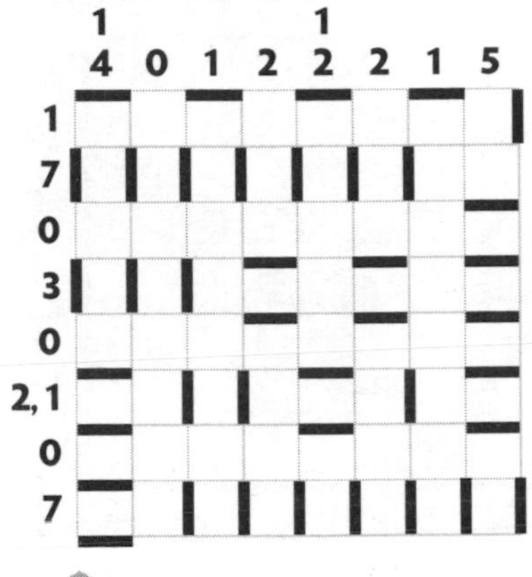

HARD

BOXING MATCH

1	2	6	2	1	7
2	3	7	3	4	8
4	5	3	2	5	1
3	5	1	4	4	2
4	2	6	5	3	7
5	3	4	3	3	2

EASY

BOXING MATCH

8	4	2	6	3	4
9	6	5	8	7	5
4	6	7	7	6	5
7	5	2	5	4	4
9	8	3	8	9	3
4	8	5	7	8	3

MEDIUM

BOXING MATCH

6	3	7	8	4	5
4	2	4	5	4	6
5	6	5	2	3	5
4	7	5	6	8	3
3	5	2	4	7	4
6	8	2	3	5	2

HARD

TARGETS

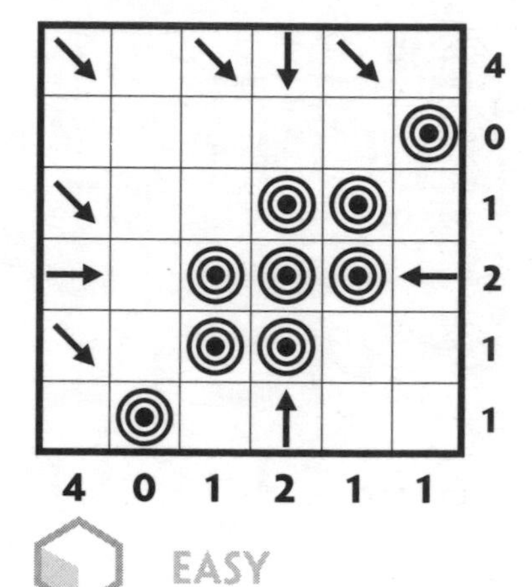

EASY

TARGETS

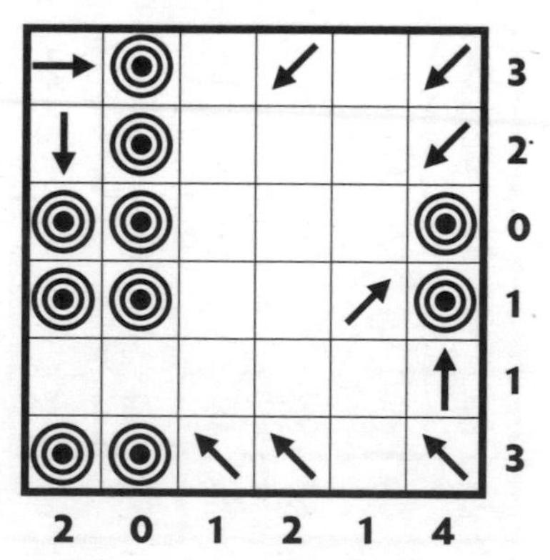

MEDIUM

TARGETS

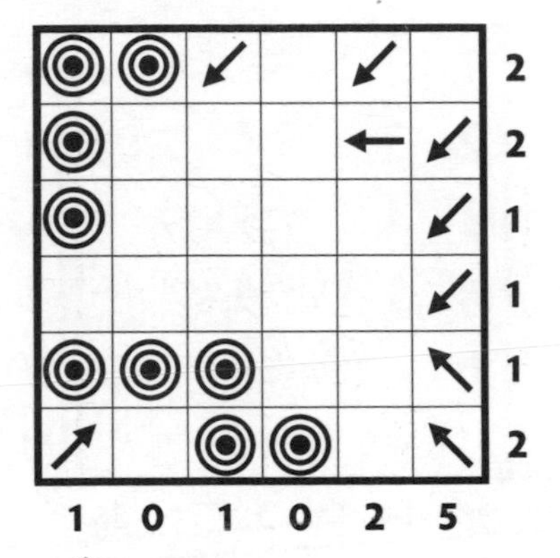

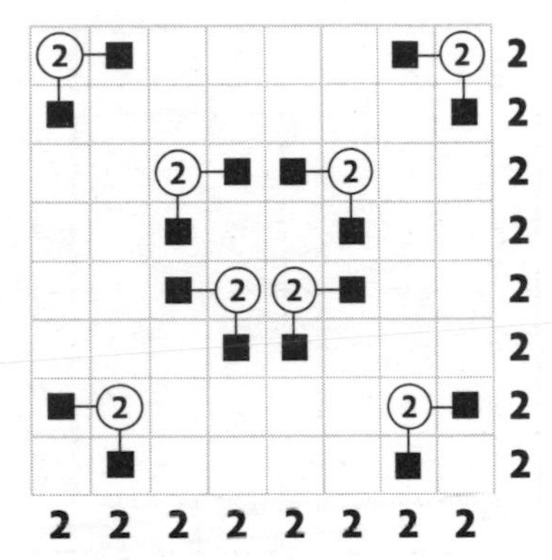

MEDIUM

BOXING MATCH

6	5	8	5	4	6
4	7	4	2	5	7
2	3	8	5	6	7
7	5	7	6	4	5
5	6	4	3	4	7
3	4	6	6	7	5

MEDIUM

CANDIES

1	2	3	4	5	6	21
						0
		4				4
	3					3
		6				6
	5					5
1	10	13	4	5	6	

EASY

CANDIES

1	2		3	4	6	16
2	3		4	5		14
3	4		5			12
4	5		6			15
6						6
		4				4
16	14	4	18	9	6	

MEDIUM

CANDIES

2	4	5	6			17
3					4	7
4					5	9
6						6
	5				6	11
	6					6
15	15	5	6	0	15	

HARD

MATH BOX

5 ⇄ 3 + 2 ⇄ 4 + 1

7 ⇅ 3 + 4 ⇅ 6 + 1

5 ⇉ 4

5 + 1 − 6

4 + 6

3 ⇄ 6

3 × 2

7 ⇅ 2

7 ⇄ 5 + 2

6 ÷ 2 ⇊ 4 − 1

7 + 1 ⇅ 5 + 3

2 ← 1 ⇄ 7 + 5 ⇄ 3 × 4

7 + 3 ⇄ 6 + 4 ⇄ 5 × 2

2 × 4 + 5 ⇉ 1 → 3 ⇉ 7 + 6

MEDIUM

BAR CODE

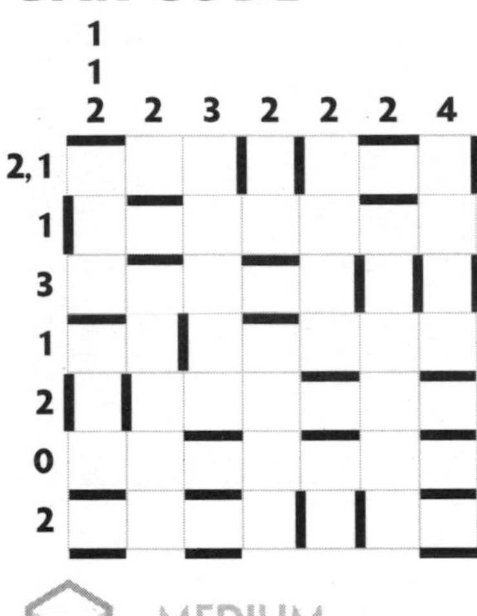

MEDIUM

ELBOW ROOM

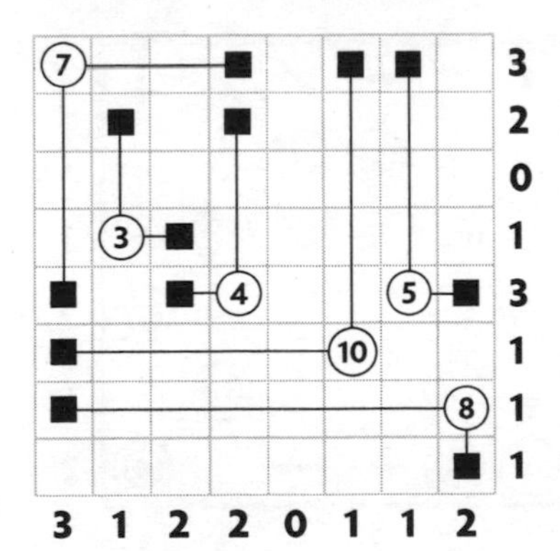

EASY

ELBOW ROOM

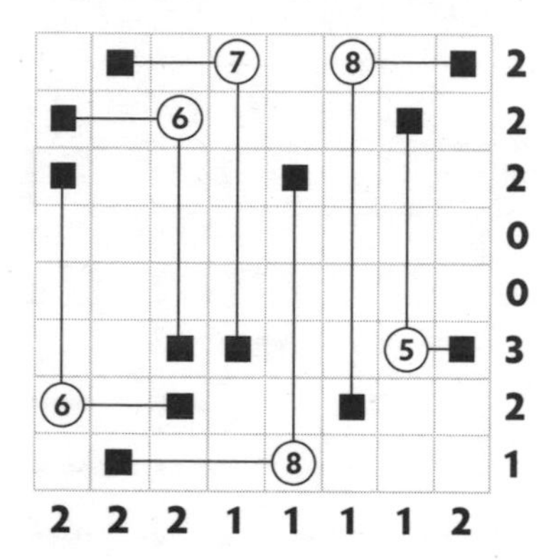

ELBOW ROOM

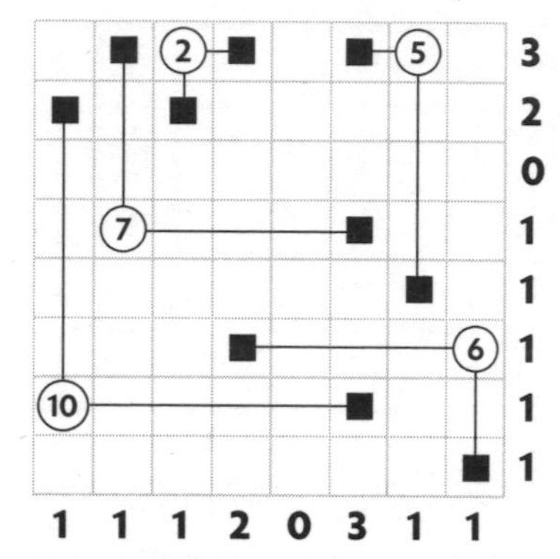

TARGETS

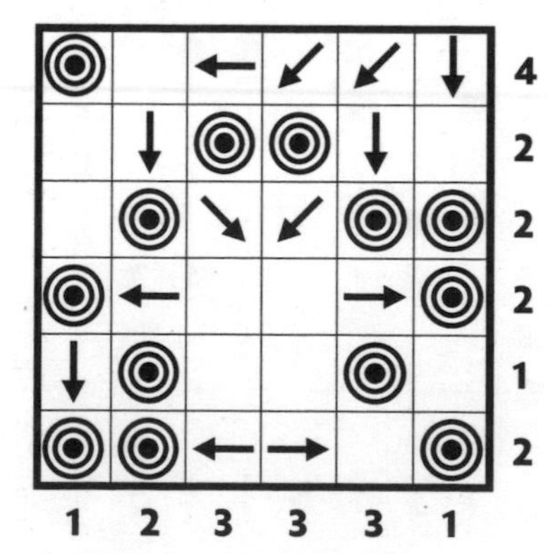

CANDIES

1					3	4
	2	3			4	9
	3			5		8
		4	5	6		15
		5	6			11
	4					4
1	9	12	11	11	7	

HARD

ELBOW ROOM

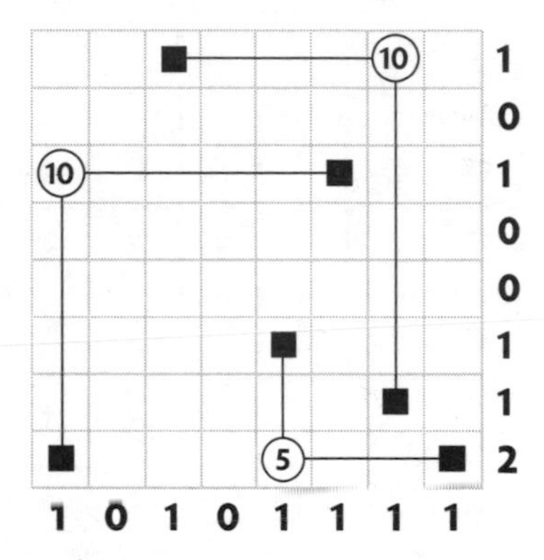

HARD

BAR CODE

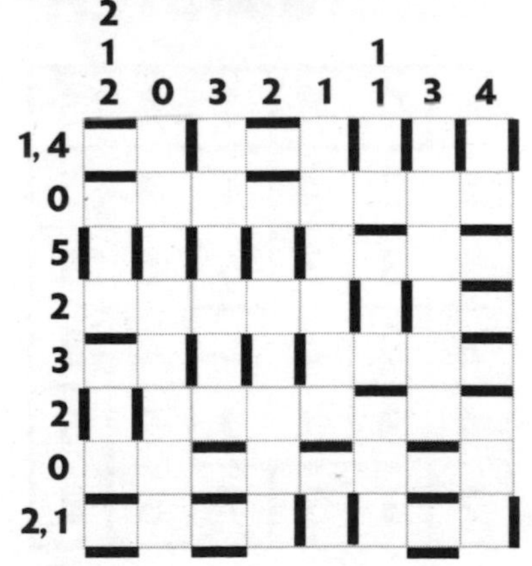

HARD

BOXING MATCH

3	4	6	8	4	3
6	5	3	7	6	5
7	8	2	1	7	3
4	5	4	9	5	1
7	5	2	8	6	4
8	6	3	2	5	4

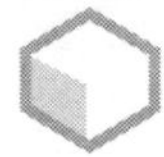

EASY

BOXING MATCH

3	4	4	5	6	4
5	7	6	3	2	1
6	5	2	6	8	7
4	3	4	6	5	4
5	6	7	3	1	2
4	6	3	4	9	8

MEDIUM

BOXING MATCH

6	9	8	3	4	5
5	2	4	3	4	5
1	3	3	6	6	5
8	9	6	5	4	3
4	3	4	2	5	5
2	3	2	7	6	4

HARD

MATH BOX

4	3	2	5	6	1
2	1	6	3	4	5
3	2	4	1	5	6
1	4	5	6	3	2
5	6	1	4	2	3
6	5	3	2	1	4

EASY

MATH BOX

4	3	1	6	5	2
1	2	4	5	6	3
3	1	5	2	4	6
2	4	6	3	1	5
6	5	2	1	3	4
5	6	3	4	2	1

MEDIUM

MATH BOX

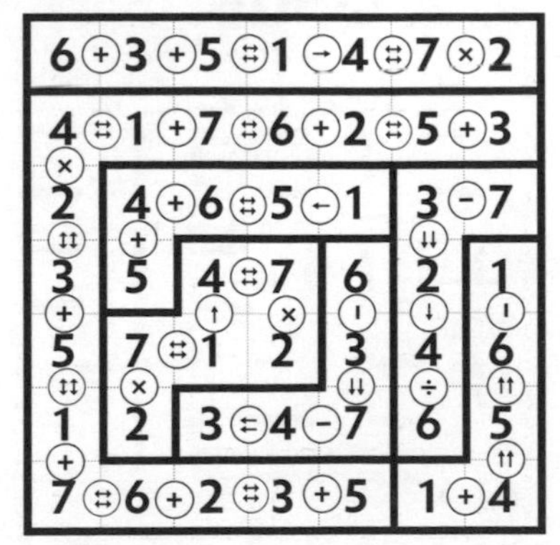

6	3	5	1	4	7	2
4	1	7	6	2	5	3
2	4	6	5	1	3	7
3	5	4	7	6	2	1
5	7	1	2	3	4	6
1	2	3	4	7	6	5
7	6	2	3	5	1	4

HARD

BAR CODE

EASY

BAR CODE

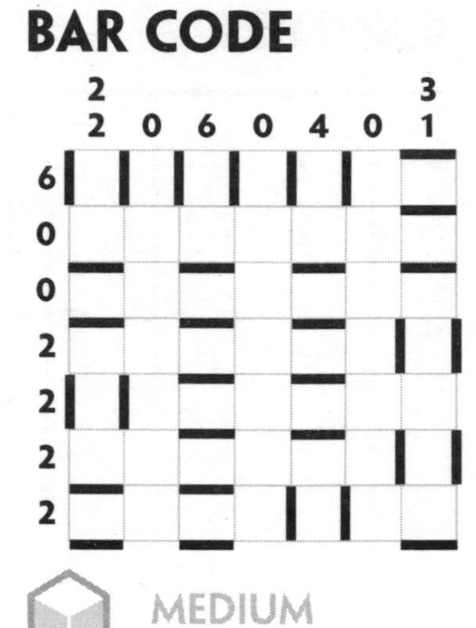

MEDIUM

BAR CODE

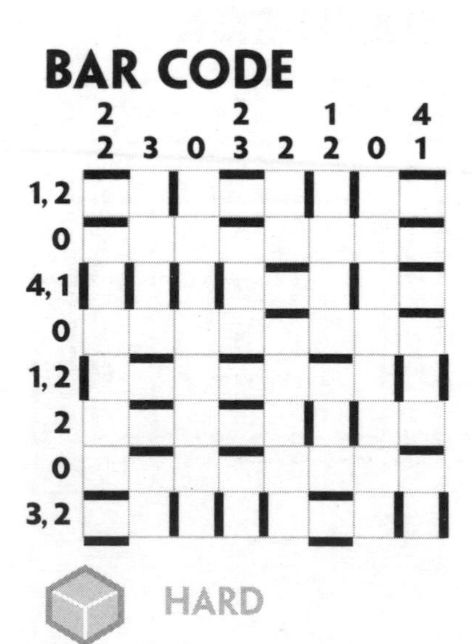

HARD

CANDIES

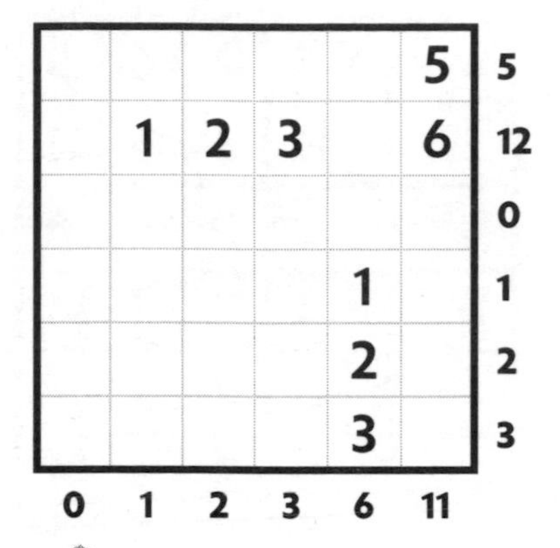

					5	5
	1	2	3		6	12
						0
				1		1
				2		2
				3		3
0	1	2	3	6	11	

EASY

CANDIES

1	2	3	4	5		15
2	3	4				9
3					4	7
	4		5		6	15
4	5		6			15
5						5
15	14	7	15	5	10	

MEDIUM

CANDIES

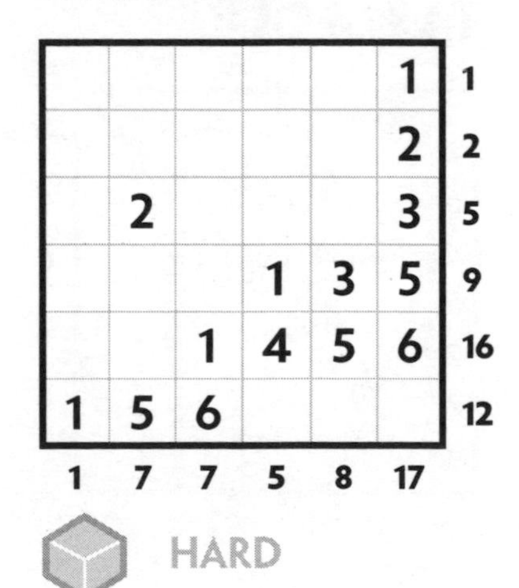

					1	1
					2	2
	2				3	5
			1	3	5	9
		1	4	5	6	16
1	5	6				12
1	7	7	5	8	17	

HARD

BAR CODE

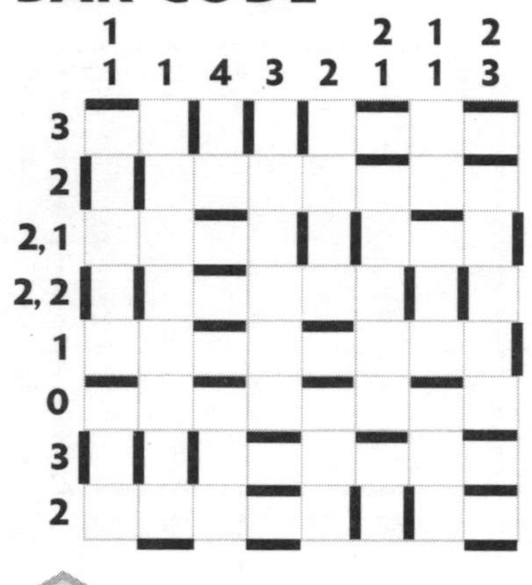

HARD

BOXING MATCH

4	6	5	2	4	5
2	4	3	3	5	4
8	6	7	9	7	6
6	5	4	4	3	4
1	2	6	2	3	7
7	5	9	8	6	8

HARD

TARGETS

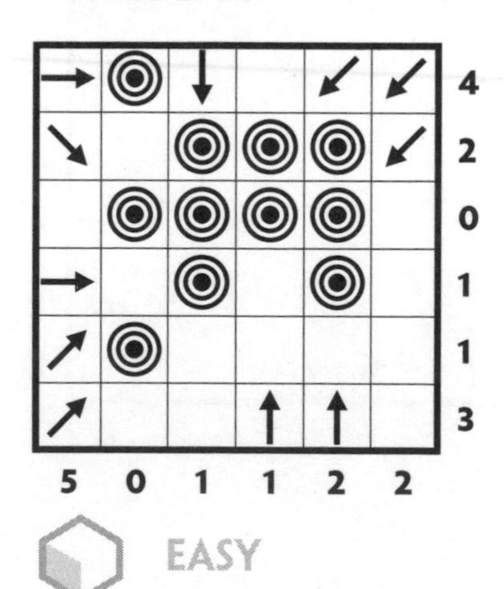

EASY

TARGETS

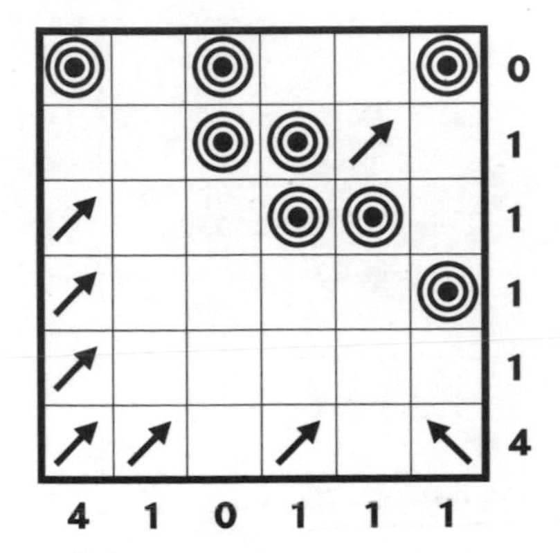

MEDIUM

TARGETS

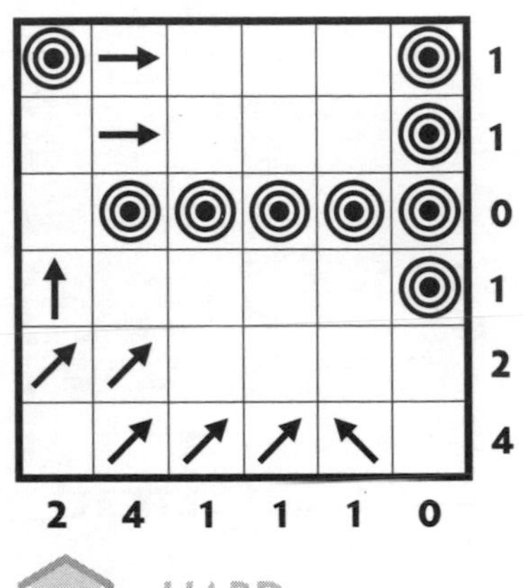

HARD

ELBOW ROOM

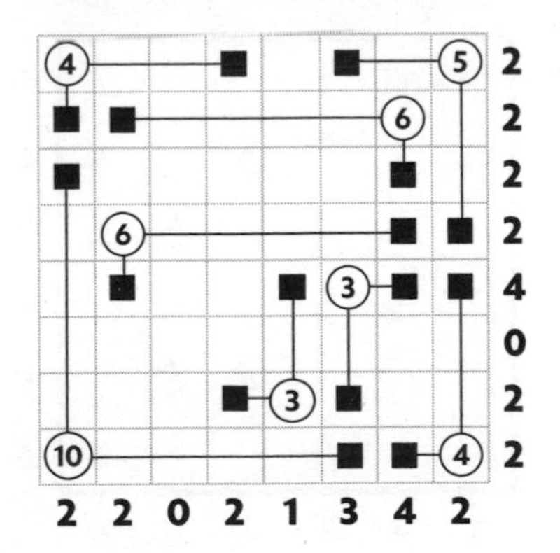

EASY

ELBOW ROOM

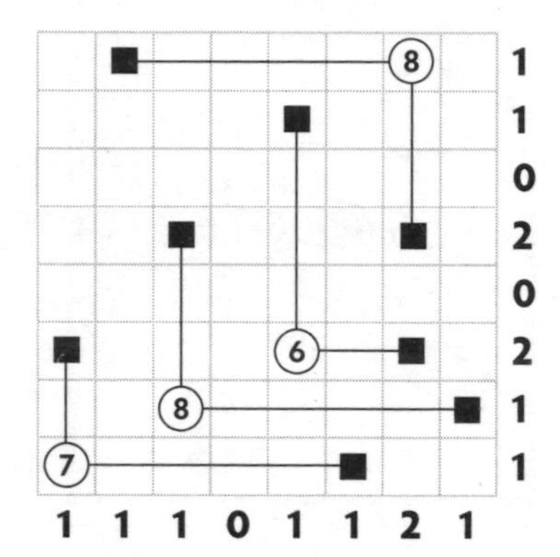

ELBOW ROOM

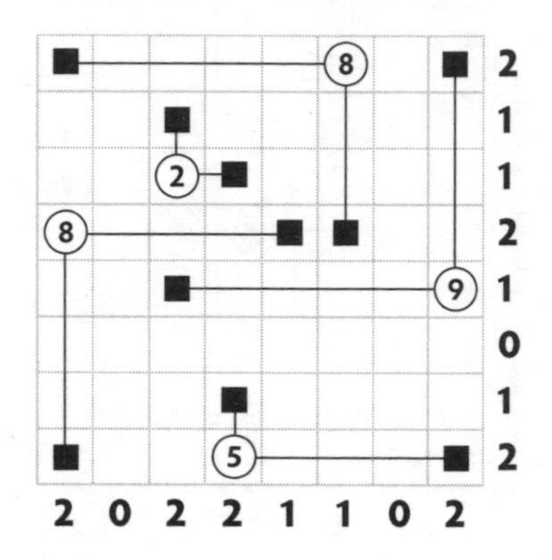

CANDIES

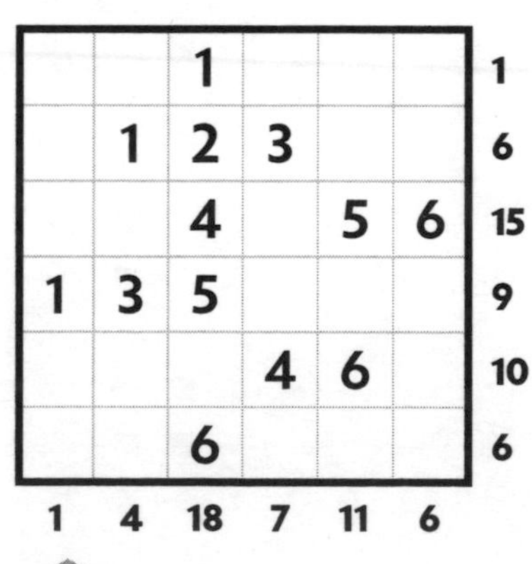

BAR CODE

Column clues: 2 1 | 2 | 2 1 | 0 | 2 | 3 | 1 3 | 3

Row clues: 1, 3, 1 | 2 | 2, 1 | 0 | 4, 1 | 0 | 5 | 0

HARD

ELBOW ROOM

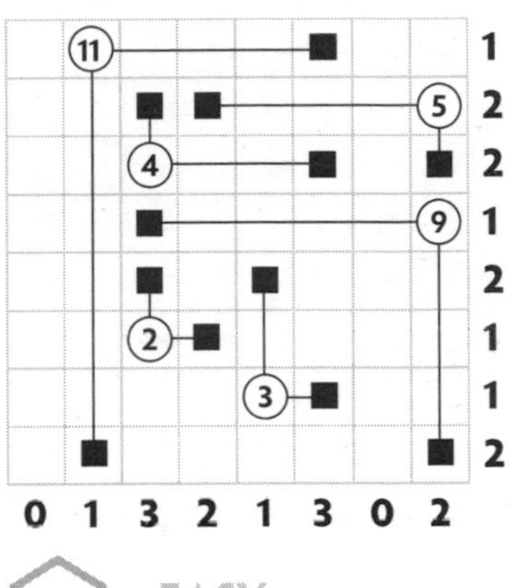

EASY

ELBOW ROOM

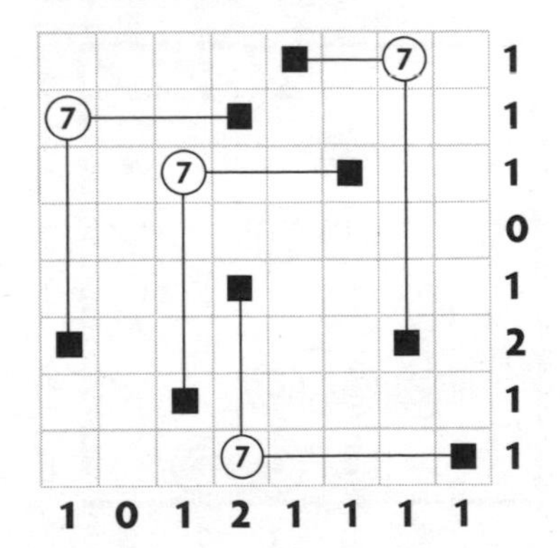

MEDIUM

ELBOW ROOM

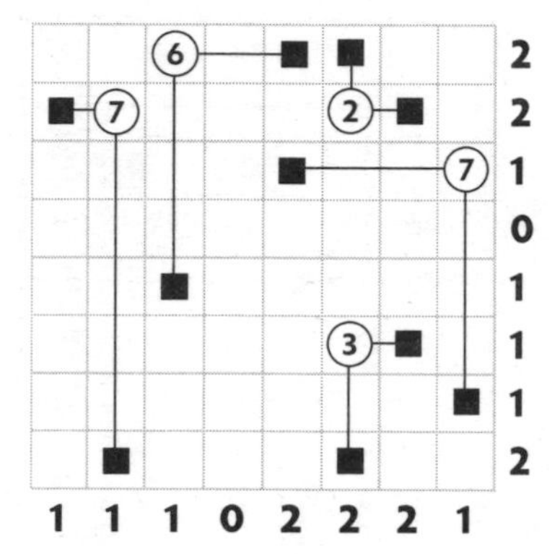

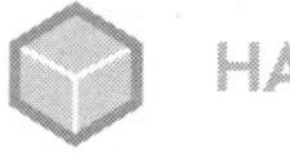
HARD

TARGETS

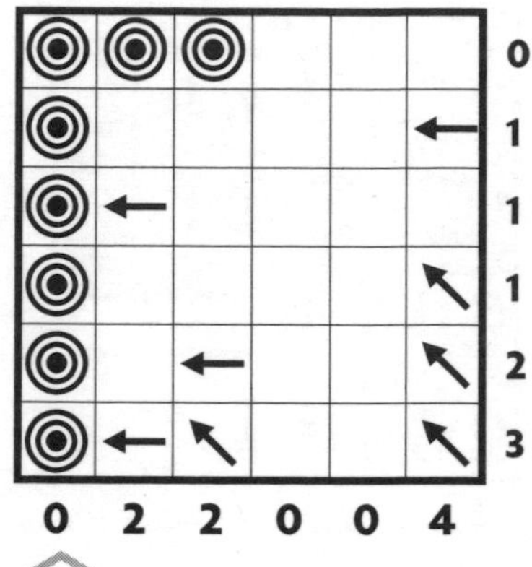

EASY

TARGETS

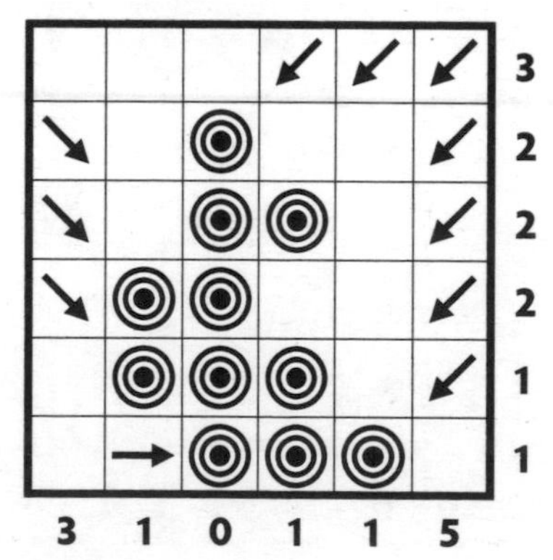

MEDIUM

TARGETS

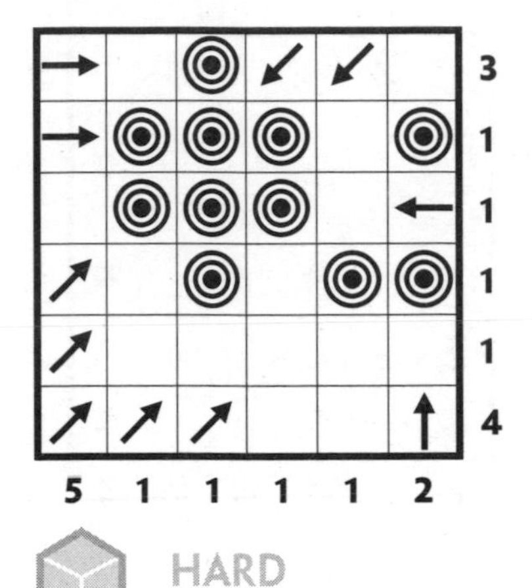

HARD

BOXING MATCH

3	4	7	4	3	5
6	5	7	2	3	8
6	5	6	9	8	7
4	2	8	5	1	6
7	4	7	3	2	8
5	6	6	8	9	7

EASY

BOXING MATCH

4	7	9	3	4	2
5	8	2	5	6	3
6	3	1	7	8	7
7	5	8	6	2	1
3	9	3	3	7	4
4	4	2	5	9	8

MEDIUM

BOXING MATCH

8	3	2	4	3	4
4	3	6	7	3	2
7	2	5	8	2	7
6	3	4	2	3	6
2	4	7	5	4	3
3	6	5	4	6	7

HARD

CANDIES

1	2			4		7
			1			1
			2			2
		3	4		5	12
2	3	4	5	6		20
4		5	6			15
7	5	12	18	10	5	

EASY

CANDIES

	1			2	3	6
2			3		4	9
3	4				5	12
5						5
6						6
	5				6	11
16	10	0	3	2	18	

MEDIUM

CANDIES

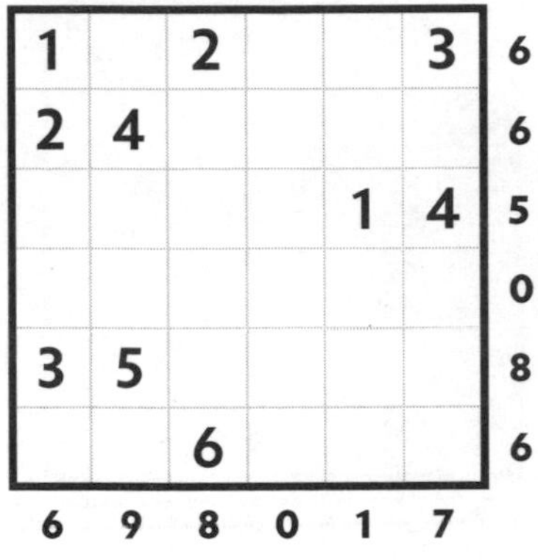

HARD

BAR CODE

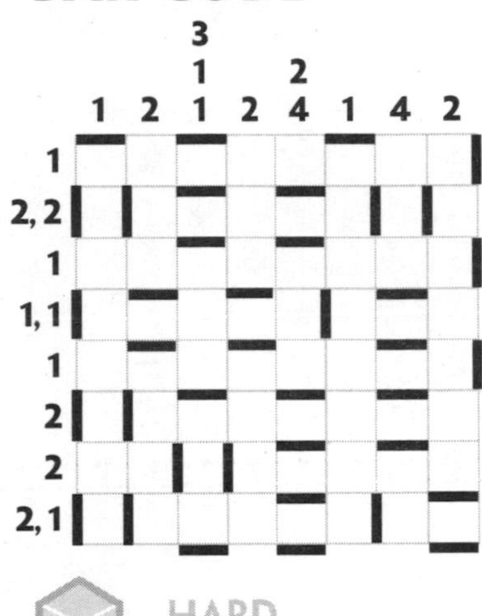

HARD

MATH BOX

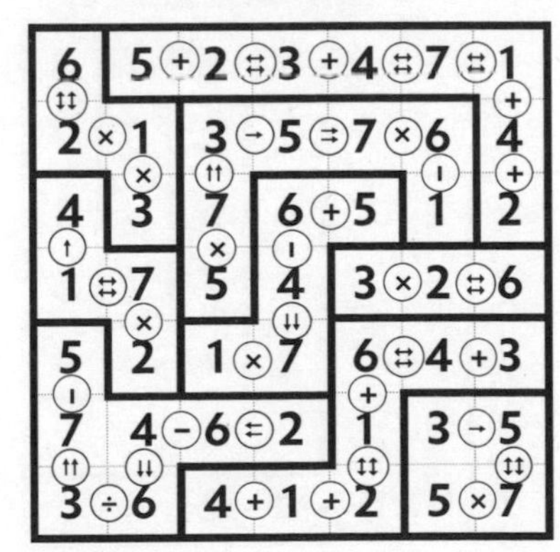

HARD

ELBOW ROOM

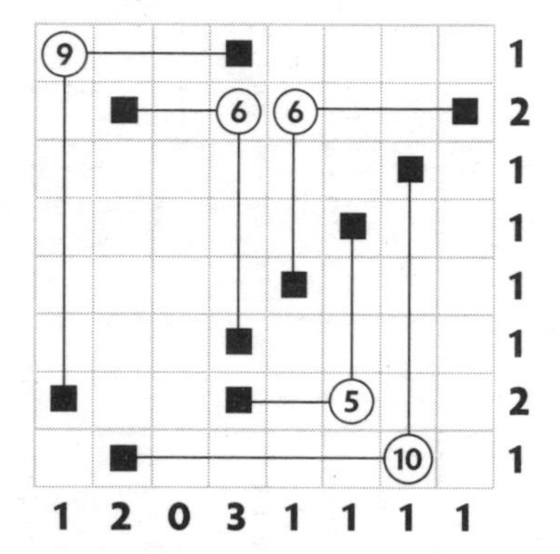

HARD

TARGETS

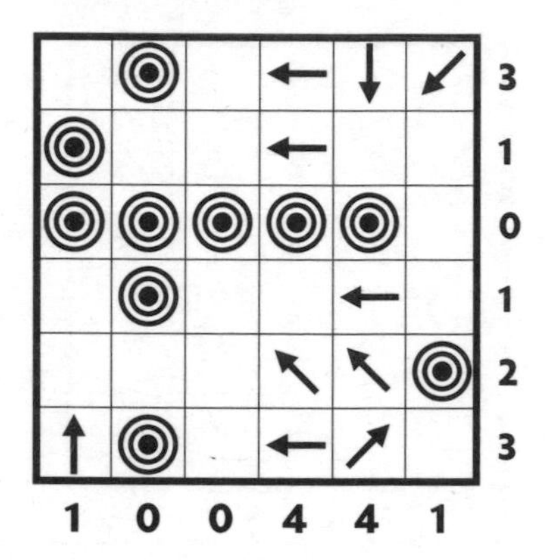

MEDIUM

MATH BOX

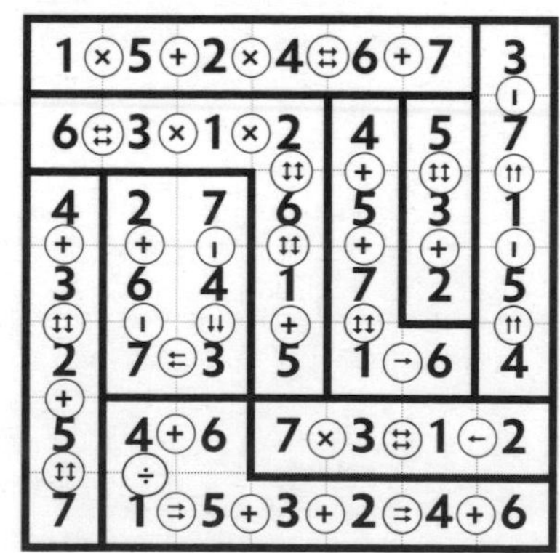

HARD

BOXING MATCH

3	6	5	4	6	7
2	4	7	5	4	3
6	5	4	2	5	6
7	4	3	8	4	5
4	3	6	7	3	2
8	5	2	4	5	4

HARD

BAR CODE

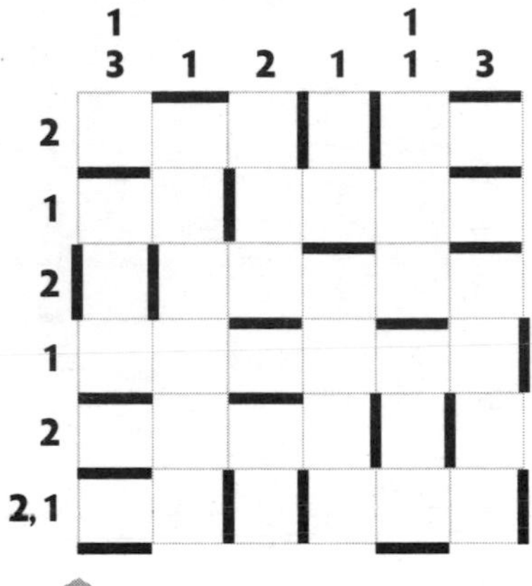

EASY

BAR CODE

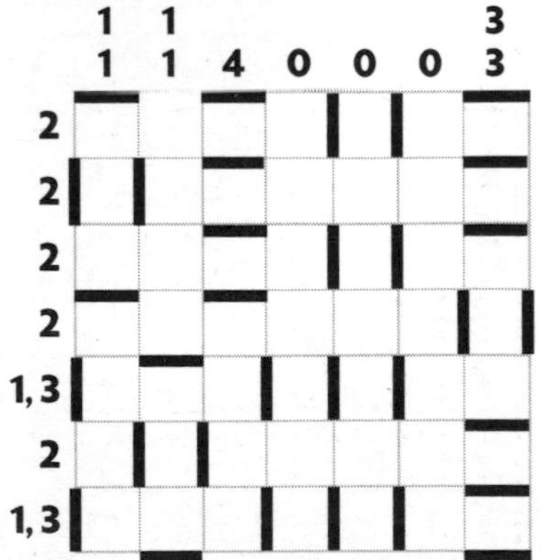

MEDIUM

BAR CODE

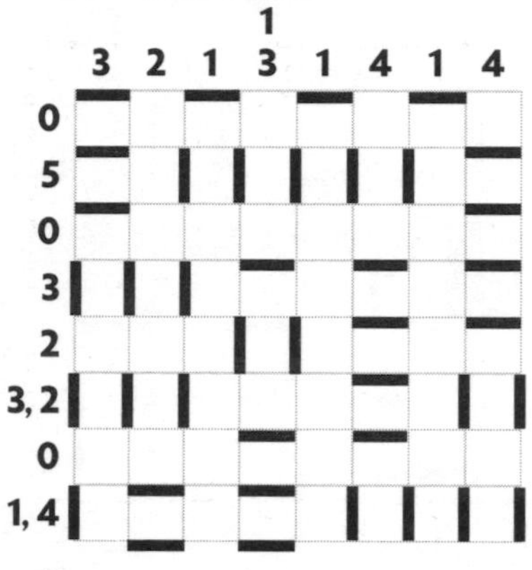

ELBOW ROOM

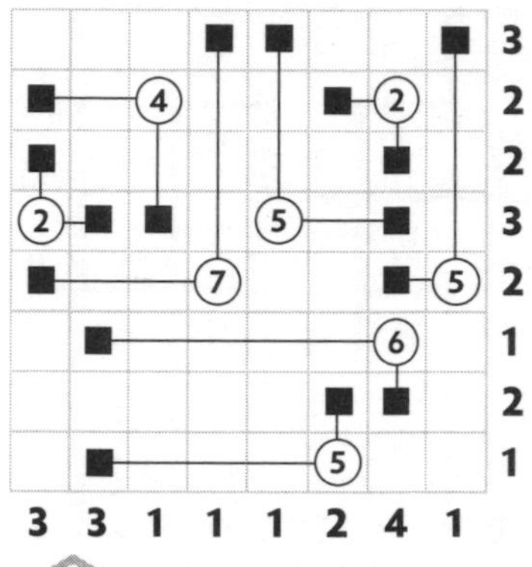

ELBOW ROOM

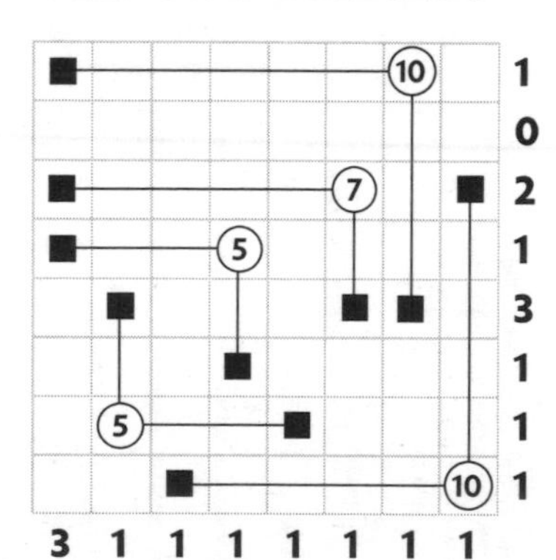

ELBOW ROOM

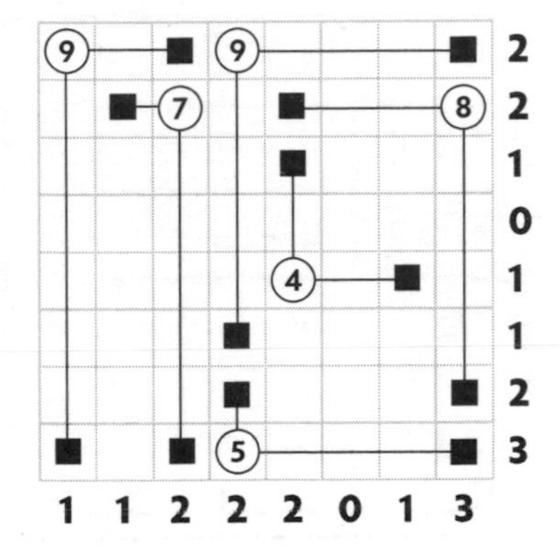

HARD

CANDIES

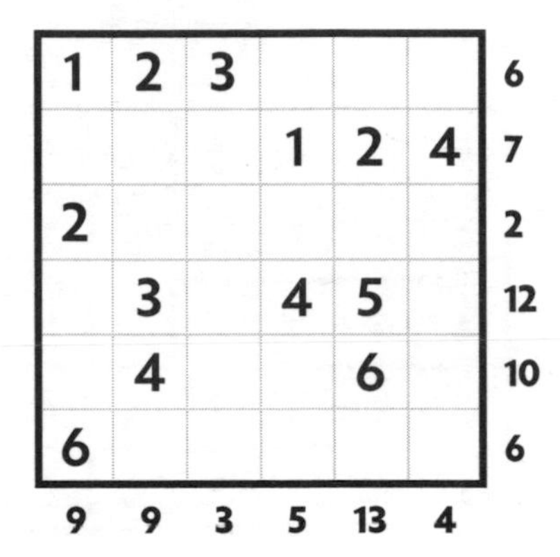

HARD

BAR CODE

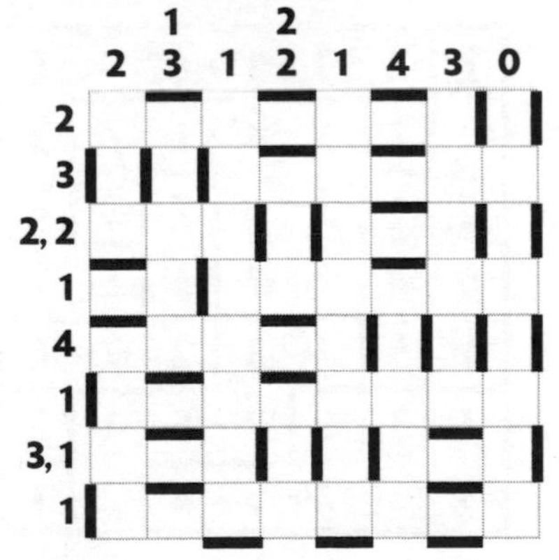

HARD

MATH BOX

1	5	3	4	6	2
3	1	4	5	2	6
4	3	2	6	5	1
2	4	6	3	1	5
6	2	5	1	3	4
5	6	1	2	4	3

EASY

MATH BOX

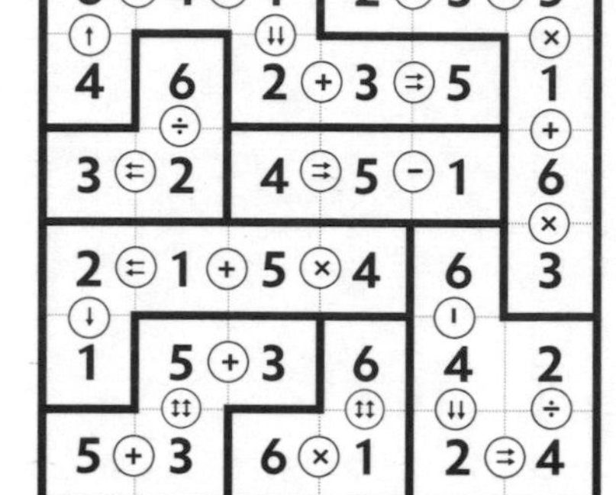

MEDIUM

MATH BOX

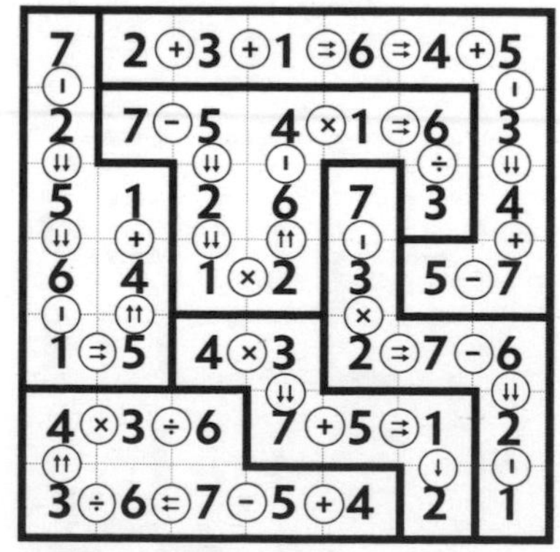

HARD

BOXING MATCH

4	6	3	1	5	4
5	4	2	8	7	3
3	6	7	3	4	5
5	2	6	2	1	7
5	1	5	8	4	6
3	4	9	3	2	7

EASY

BOXING MATCH

2	3	4	5	3	6
4	6	6	1	4	5
5	1	2	5	3	1
3	2	4	6	2	6
5	5	6	2	3	5
4	1	3	4	3	2

MEDIUM

BOXING MATCH

4	6	5	2	4	5
2	4	3	3	5	4
8	6	7	9	7	6
6	5	4	4	3	4
1	2	6	2	3	7
7	5	9	8	6	8

HARD

ELBOW ROOM

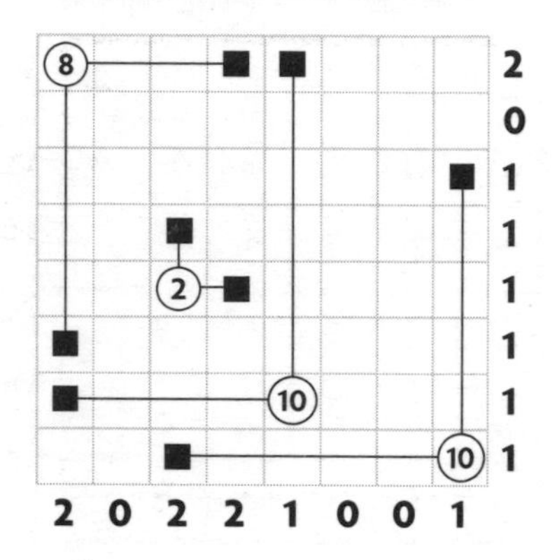

HARD

BAR CODE

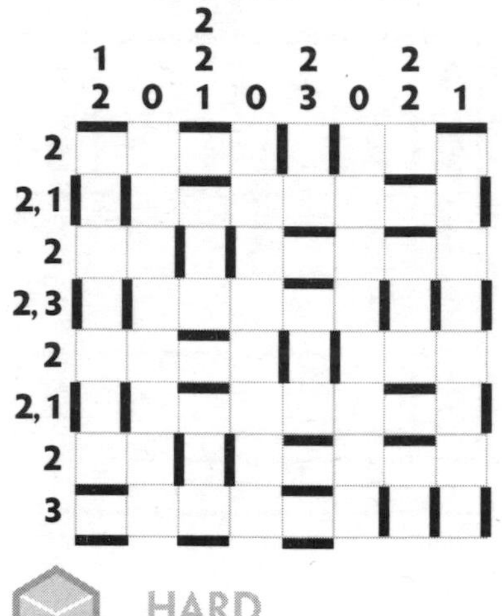

HARD

CANDIES

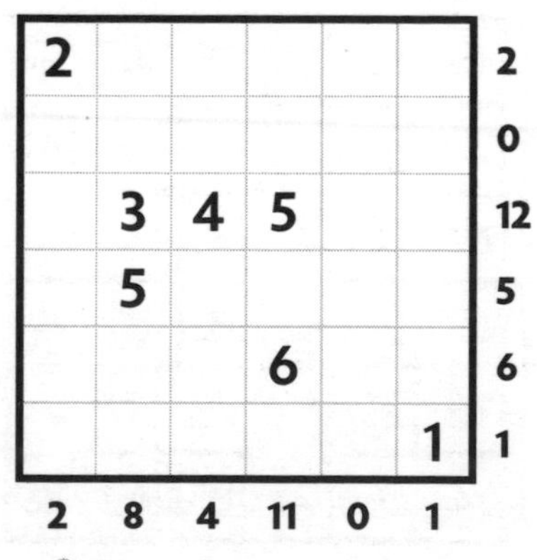

EASY

CANDIES

1		2	3	4	5	15
2	3		6			11
3		4		5	6	18
4						4
		5		6		11
5		6				11
15	3	17	9	15	11	

MEDIUM

CANDIES

3					4	7
	1	2	3	4	5	15
	2	3	4	5		14
	3	4				7
4	5	6				15
5	6					11
12	17	15	7	9	9	

HARD

BOXING MATCH

5	6	5	6	8	7
4	7	2	1	9	1
3	8	3	5	4	2
7	7	2	8	9	4
6	5	2	3	7	1
4	6	4	6	2	3

HARD

MATH BOX

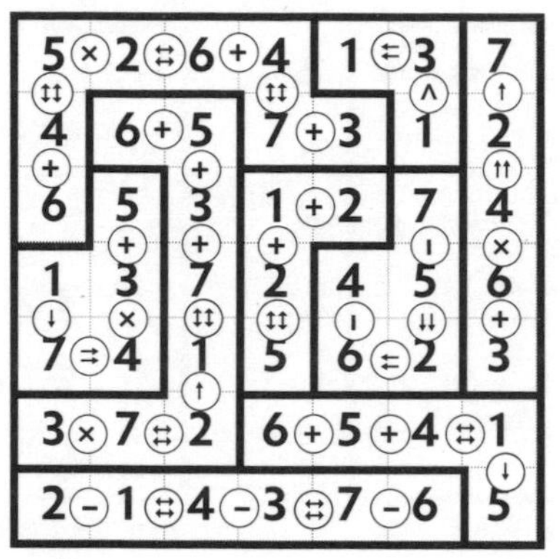

HARD

YOUR NOTES

YOUR NOTES